P

Vice-Chancellor and Officers
to Members of Staff

to mark the

50th Anniversary
of Cranfield University

October 1996

Field of Vision

The first fifty years of Cranfield University

By Revel Barker

Designed by Sterling Design Ltd
Typeset and printed by Sterling Press Ltd

First published in 1996 by
Cranfield University Press
Cranfield
Bedfordshire

Reprinted August 1996

ISBN 1 871315 60 3

The University of Wharley End

WHARLEY End, in the parish of Cranfield, on Bedfordshire's Buckinghamshire border, sounds like the stuff of Victorian melodrama and is difficult to find on any but the largest scale map. Apparently once a clearing for hogs, and presumably beside a field with cranes, of the ornithological type, it is almost equi-distant between London and Birmingham, and between Oxford and Cambridge, and sits conveniently between two junctions of the M1 motorway. But there are no signs to warn that you are entering it, only a pair of 30mph speed limit warnings, and a clue on the corner that says Wharley End Garage. The village has a mosque but no church, it has a playschool but no village school, and a bank offering a full international service that is open five full days a week. It also has a supermarket, a Post Office, a bookshop, a library, its own fire brigade, a gent's hairdresser and a dental surgery. A high proportion of the residents is educated to at least first-degree level, and many emanate from overseas.

It also has an airport, with frequent international flights. And it has one of the world's leading post-graduate institutions of engineering, technology and management, which happily takes its name from the parish in which it is based, rather than from the precise geographical location. It actually takes its name from RAF Cranfield, a pre-war and wartime aerodrome which, in 1946, was adapted by an enlightened government to become a post-graduate College of Aeronautics, and to help convert the formidable range of aeronautical inventions developed rapidly in the first half of the forties to commercial and peacetime advantage. The Royal Air Force habit is to adopt the name of the village round the back of the airfield, rather than the one next to the front gate, where the housing and administrative blocks are based.

The College of Aeronautics was founded at Cranfield by people who believed passionately in the importance of aviation in both war and peace. In 1946 Sir Frederick Handley Page said: "without research and education in aeronautics we shall no longer be in the forefront of nations." The founding fathers had vivid memories of the Battle of Britain and believed that there were few things more vital to the country than a flourishing aircraft industry. In the war years Britain had been a world leader in military aviation but, by the end of the war America was challenging that lead with obvious implications for civil aviation in times of peace.

Fifty years later, Cranfield's list of clients, sponsors and associated companies included Aeroflot, Alitalia, Boeing,

Bofors, British Aerospace, British Airways, Dassault, Fokker, Lufthansa, Messerschmitt-Bolkow-Blohm, Nasa, most of the world's leading airlines and the governments and defence ministries of most friendly nations.

Meanwhile, Cranfield had reached out to other villages: to nearby Silsoe (said by some to be the most famous village in the world, after that other agricultural community, Ambridge), where the School of Agriculture, Food and Environment, including the Soil Survey and Land Research Centre, is located, and to Old Warden village, where Shuttleworth College, part of the School, is located.

Yet another village is Shrivenham, at the far western end of the Vale of the White Horse in Oxfordshire. Shrivenham is home to the Royal Military College of Science, which traces its roots back via Woolwich to 1772, where Cranfield was contracted to provide the academic and research staff and resources for Britain's fast-track military technicians and for defence related clients, military and civilian, from friendly nations in all parts of the world. And recently the University stretched to a city, to Gloucester where, with the Royal Gloucester Hospital, it has established a Post-graduate Centre of Medical Sciences.

The impact of these small villages on the world's wealth has been tremendous. Aircraft that are household names, Concorde and the Harrier to name only two, have been aided in their development at Wharley End, and there is no Rolls-Royce engine that has not been improved there;

scientists have left Silsoe to find water for the third world, or have stayed there to make farms more productive worldwide; Shrivenham has invented the first-ever substitute for gunpowder, trained United Nations inspectors to detect biological and chemical warfare factories, and has taught countries how to prepare for disaster, whether natural or man-made. In management, Cranfield is rated second on a world scale.

The Harrier,

redeveloped

at Cranfield

The impact of a world player on these villages has, in a similar manner, also been enormous. Cranfield is a major employer in Bedfordshire, and also an indirect employer, because the bulk of its services are procured locally rather than nationally. The Cranfield site alone is a

£60million per annum operation. It has more than 1,500 students on campus at any one time, at least one-third of whom come from outside the United Kingdom, about half from other EU countries and the rest from outside Europe. Their average age, because in addition to a first degree they also often bring experience in the world of industry or commerce, is 29, and consequently many bring families with them; some live in the former RAF married quarters on campus, others prefer to rent accommodation in the local community. The students therefore have an impact on the local community far greater than the effect of an undergraduate-focused university might be.

In the mid-nineties they spend something more than £10million per annum. A significant number of pupils at the Lower School in Cranfield village are the children of Cranfield students, many of them from overseas. They create opportunities and greatly enrich the local schools, coming from families who are the future leaders in their own countries and families in which education is greatly valued. Most years there will be twenty or more different nationalities in the village school – which must provide an enormous advantage to the teaching of geography, as well as to the understanding of social integration.

In addition to its own activities, Cranfield campus also provides a base for other organisations whose activities relate to those of the University – the British Hydromechanics Research Group, the British Aerospace

Manufacturing Group, Cranfield Impact Centre (which designs crash resistance for the world's car manufacturers), various airfield related companies, and Nissan's European Technology Centre, where all the Nissan cars destined for the European market are designed for manufacture in Washington Co Durham and in Spain.

The University's academic staff at Cranfield, most of whom are experienced in industry or commerce as well as in education, is bolstered by a further 650 people who work on the campus, who live in the local community, and whose spending power sustains a large number of local businesses and jobs.

The sites at Shrivenham, Silsoe and Shuttleworth, although not as large as Cranfield, also have a major influence on their local economy. The School of Agriculture Food and Environment, for example, employs 300 people directly; it is a £12million per annum business, with about 700 under- or post-graduate students who inject a further £2.5million into the local economy every year.

Whatever the impact locally, a place like Silsoe or like Shrivenham, or even like Wharley End, will never lose its identity, although nowadays they each have an alternative choice, like a married name, for they are also Cranfield University. This, then, is that story.

I am indebted, in the compilation of this short history, to several people: to Peter Donnelly for compiling most of the research; to University archivist John Harrington, of course, for providing an overview of the history and for access to numerous documents including the early annual reports; to Vice-Chancellors Lord Chilver and Frank Hartley and to Deputy Vice-Chancellor Ron Fletcher for their particular views of the history; to P A (Phil) Digger for his reminiscences, to Derek Mitchell, to Mrs Bernice Maynard of Cranfield village, an amateur historian only in the sense that she works unpaid, and especially to the Chancellor, Lord Kings Norton of Wotton Underwood, for his amazing recollections of an amazing life.

Any unattributed opinions are nevertheless my own, as are any mistakes.

Revel Barker, Wharley End, January 1996.

Field of Vision

VISITORS to Cranfield in the summer of 1944 were unlikely to be deeply impressed with one aspect of the in-depth research work being carried out there: teams of dedicated men, all wearing darkened goggles, pedalling furiously around the barrack square on Walls and Eldorado stop-me-and-buy-one ice-cream tricycles.

They were, inquiries would reveal, RAF fighter pilots intent on improving their night flying vision and, with a war far from won, that seemed the most sensible and economical way of so doing.

Yet from such bizarre beginnings grew one of the world's most respected and renowned centres of learning, at the forefront of aerospace technology and research, and with an international reputation for excellence in the fields of technology, engineering, applied science, manufacturing, management, defence and agriculture.

But the story of Cranfield University begins the summer before those pilots were seen at their curious night-flying exercises. "Before the War was over," the Chancellor, Lord Kings Norton, recalls, "there was a great deal of interest in post-war education, not least in aeronautics. In 1943 we knew we were going to win, and that we should be preparing for the post-war era.

That summer the Royal Aeronautical Society, of which the Chancellor – then Dr Harold Roxbee Cox – was a vice-president, organised an historic two-day conference at which he took the chair. The main item on the agenda was a method of organising the education of Britain's post-war aeronautical elite. One of the moving spirits, then and later, was Sir Roy Fedden.

Fedden, a brilliant aero-engine designer, had helped make the Bristol Aeroplane Company the world's leading engine producer in the Thirties, and in 1942 became Special Technical Adviser to the Minister of Aircraft Production.

A new Minister, Sir Stafford Cripps, asked Fedden to head an extended fact-finding mission to the United States to discover everything and anything that Britain could learn from America about aircraft production and design.

Fedden's team returned to produce a massive and extraordinarily comprehensive seven-part report, one section of which dealt solely with education and pinpointed, as "the high spot of the whole tour", visits to the Institutes of Technology in Massachusetts and in California, where the researchers had been particularly impressed.

British industrialists, though, were quick to pour scorn on the mission's findings. They doubted that Great Britain could learn anything of value from the Americans, and took particular exception to the claim that, compared to the United States, British companies were drastically short of qualified engineers,

They dubbed the report "Fedden's Folly", but Sir Stafford Cripps thought quite the opposite. It was, he declared enthusiastically, "undoubtedly the greatest single volume that has been written about a single industry."

It was against that controversial background that Roxbee Cox chaired two open meetings of the Royal Aeronautical Society on June 25 and July 23, 1943. Their theme: "The education and training of aeronautical engineers."

Leading figures in the industry, including Sir Frederick Handley Page, were among the speakers, but the most significant contributions came from Professor Sir Melvill Jones, Chairman of the Aeronautical Research Council – the Government's chief advisory body on aeronautical affairs – and, vitally, Fedden.

Both speakers strongly advocated the need for specialist post-graduate aeronautical education, and within a month, on August 10, 1943, the Research Council produced a follow-up report outlining the way forward.

It proposed the setting up of a central post-graduate aeronautical school, whose principal subjects would include aerodynamics, structures, propulsion, design and construction.

The school should provide two-year courses, as well as short courses, but with no undergraduates. More precisely, entry was to be of post-graduate or post-experience standard. Post-experience meant that some students could be admitted with academic qualifications below degree level provided they had some equivalent valuable experience in industry. All students would be given scholarships.

Research establishments would be required to co-operate and to exchange staff, made up at the school of a Principal, four professors, eight to ten senior lecturers, a flight superintendent and junior staff.

The school, it was decided, should be affiliated to a university and have its own airfield and aircraft, and be financed by the State.

It was a tall order, but Fedden was equal to the task. His system of influencing his minister was to take advantage of the long journeys they made together by car, and that is how he was eventually able to persuade Cripps to let him start putting those plans into practice.

That October, Fedden was appointed chairman of an inter-departmental committee charged with "preparing and submitting to the Minister of Aircraft Production detailed proposals for a School of Aeronautical Science."

The committee went to work at once, meeting sixteen times and collecting a mass of evidence from leading figures in the aeronautical industry. By July 1944 it was able to submit a report called "A College of Aeronautics".

It included the declaration: "We were not charged with examining the case for such a college. We have taken it for granted." Now commonly known as The Fedden Report, it was the blueprint for Cranfield.

The Fedden Report largely accepted the earlier Aeronautical Research Council recommendations, with one important exception: Fedden proposed that the new college should be totally independent of any other education body, having its own board of governors, and should be financed by a grant from the Ministry of Education, rather than through the University Grants Committee.

Not surprisingly, in view of the amount of the sometimes contradictory evidence collected, some of the detailed provisions show differences in emphasis. Fedden's biographer, Bill Gunston, suggests that three editions of the report were written – one by Fedden himself and then two successive rewrites, incorporating modifications in emphasis and phrasing, by civil servants. Whatever, the outcome appears as something of a compromise between Fedden's ambitions and the more cautious view of the civil servants.

The primary plan envisaged by the report called for a new, purpose-built college, equipped from the outset at a level not far below that of existing research establishments. The cost of this plan was estimated at £2.61million, with an annual recurrent cost of £360,000. Too ambitious, probably; too costly, certainly. But the way to ensure achieving the aim was to put in an outrageous proposal against which a less ambitious plan would appear astonishingly economic, and this the report did. It went on to detail a second, "short-term", "compromise" proposal which, instead of providing for new buildings, suggested that the college could be located in a converted air station.

This more conservative solution was costed at a mere £200,000 and the austere climate in which Britain found itself in 1945 ensured that this second solution would be the one adopted.

Even so, the constant criticism which Fedden had faced from the outset was not silenced. Cranfield archivist John Harrington says: "Some academics from existing universities were hostile to what they saw as Fedden's concept for a British equivalent of an American-style super Institute of Technology, which would be independent of the University Grants Committee system.

"The most vitriolic critics of all, however, were aircraft industrialists, who lobbied Sir Stafford Cripps for three years, claiming the proposed post-graduate college would be 'a white elephant', an 'unwanted monstrosity' and a 'useless burden'.

In all, Cripps received formal protests from 24 academics and 18 industrialists, but his continued support for the

College from 1944 onwards and through his ministerial influence on Atlee's first post-war Labour Government was to prove crucial.

So, despite the storm of protest and criticism, the Government accepted the Fedden Report's compromise proposals, and the search for a suitable site for the new college began.

The report suggested three possible locations: Harwell, where the Atomic Energy Authority was to be based; Watchfield, a grass runway strip which, by coincidence, is adjacent to Cranfield's operation at RMCS Shrivenham; and Cranfield, home of the Empire Test Pilots' School, close to both Cardington and the Royal Aircraft Establishment at Bedford, and only about an hour's drive out of London.

"Harwell was the first proposition for the site", recalls Lord Kings Norton, an original member of the Board of Governors, "and that was dropped for some reason. But of course the obvious place was the old Empire Test Pilots' School, which had all the adjuncts of an aeronautical centre. So we took that, and Cranfield started, very appropriately, with an airfield."

———

THE RAF AIRFIELD at Cranfield had opened on June 1, 1937, under the control of No 1 (Bomber) Group, and the following month became the base of 62 and 68 Squadrons and their Hawker Hind bi-planes.

These were replaced by Blenheim I's early the following year and, says Michael J.F. Bowyer in *Action Stations 6: Military Airfields of the Cotswolds and Central Midlands,* "September's Munich crisis brought them to high readiness, with hazardous allotted tasks including attacks on German power resources."

In August, 1939, 62 Squadron was ordered to Singapore, where it would be decimated in the struggle against the Japanese invasion of 1941-42. Meanwhile at Cranfield work went on through the winter of 1939-40 to replace its grass airstrip with three properly-surfaced hard runways.

They became the targets of enemy attacks in the late summer of 1940, during the Battle of Britain. The first bombing came on the night of August 27-28, when incendiary and high explosive bombs were dropped to the north and south of the airfield. The following month a parachute mine exploded in a nearby field, damaging houses and shops in Cranfield High Street.

Then on October 13 a mine, complete with parachute, was found hanging from a tree in Hulcote Wood, south of the airfield, where it was thought to have dropped three weeks earlier. Bomb explosive experts quickly exploded it but, says Bowyer, "a story went round camp that the detonation brought about by the Station Armament Officer had demolished a ceiling in his house!"

Another drama came that winter, when a pupil pilot landed an Oxford after his instructor was wounded by a German intruder. But the hero of Cranfield of 1940 was Aircraftman Vivienne Hollowday who twice, in July and August, risked his life battling to save crew from blazing crashed aircraft.

For his double acts of gallantry in trying to save the airmen, who lie in the churchyard of Cranfield village, he was awarded the George Cross.

In August 1941, No 51 Operational Training Unit opened at the airfield, offering night fighter crews courses, mainly with Blenheims, and assumed such major importance that Cranfield acquired a satellite at Twinwood, north of Bedford, where Blenheim Vs were introduced early in 1942.

In the summer of 1944, Cranfield provided a visual feast for Michael Bowyer: "As our Oxford R6350 circled", he wrote, "it was clear that Cranfield was an aircraft enthusiast's paradise.

"Grouped on the south side were 100 Spitfires in varied hues and many forms. Scattered among them were 15 Typhoons and about 50 Mustang 111s, many conspicuously wearing 'invasion stripes'. Towards the north-east corner of the airfield rested Mosquito 11s, the first of which had joined 51 OTU in July. Close by were 10 Beauforts and a fine assortment of Beaufighter 1s and VIs..."

And there, too, were those ice cream pilots: "Stop me and buy one? Impossible", wrote the playful Bowyer, "yet here was a crowd of RAF pilots – or impressed ice cream men –

propelling Walls and Eldorado tricycles around Cranfield's barrack square.

"It was summertime, so dark glasses were not incongruous But, surely, something must be wrong? Nobody joined the Air Force to sell ice cream. 'We're not selling ice creams on a night fighter station in the middle of a war far from won. We're improving our night vision – under orders. Didn't you guess?' Well, yes, I was cheating a bit. I had heard of this curious activity for which Cranfield was well known..."

The theory behind the goggles was that if pilots were denied peripheral light by wearing flying goggles with dark red lenses their eye muscles would be strengthened and their night vision improved. Pilots were required to wear them for at least 20 minutes in the parade ground during the day, every day, while operational. The thinking behind the trikes was that the aircrew should be made to practise manoeuvres, while so disadvantaged – and that these highly skilled, and highly valuable, airmen were less likely to come to harm on three wheels than on two.

Immediately following the barrack square exercise they were allowed to remove the goggles and sent to a specially-darkened gymnasium to play games like table tennis and handball using white bats and balls. They also played football, with one side wearing white shorts and the other white singlets.

The pilots were reissued with the goggles and required to wear them at night for at least 20 minutes in the Briefing

Room, so that their eyes quickly adapted to the darkness when they went out into the night. And to simulate a night situation there were other darkened rooms, with moonlight and starlight conditions, where aircraft recognition exercises were carried out.

At the end of the War No 51 OTU was disbanded, and by the end of June, 1945, their last Mosquitoes, Beaufighters and Beauforts were flown away. But flying returned to Cranfield within months, when the Empire Test Pilots' School transferred there from Boscombe Down in November.

The first ETPS course began at Cranfield in January 1946, and post-war needs for test pilots in Britain and around the world were increasingly met by its graduates. But, says Bowyer, "having them closer to the latest developments in aviation and testing techniques was desirable, so ETPS moved to Farnborough in August, 1947." There had been periods when RAF Cranfield seemed ready for closure...

———

FAR from it, though. The future of Cranfield had already been decided and, after the Government accepted Fedden's compromise proposals, a Board of Governors was appointed under the chairmanship of Air Chief Marshal Sir Edgar Ludlow-Hewitt. They met for the first time on Wednesday June 28, 1945, and the Chancellor recalls the people of great eminence he joined that day:

"The governors present included Sir Roy Fedden, the great designer of the famous Bristol radial engines; Sir Frederick Handley Page, head of the great aircraft firm which bore his name; Mr J.D. North, the extraordinary polymath who headed the then well-known aircraft firm Boulton-Paul; Professor Sir Melvill Jones, the leading aeronautical scientist of his day; and Sir Harold Hartley, a multi-discipline scientist of great contemporary distinction.

"The Board of Governors had the initial tasks of finding a Principal, appointing the first Professors and staff and preparing Cranfield for its new task. Those early days were not without trouble, but we got off to a fairly good start."

First the Board set up three committees responsible for building, staffing and finance. As recommended by Fedden, the College received funding directly from the Ministry of Education in the form of an annual grant-in-aid (£3,126 9s 11d for the period from December 1945 to the end of March, 1946, followed by £271,740 for the year ending March, 1947).

They selected fifty-eight-year-old Professor E.F. (Ernest) Relf, a distinguished and experienced aerodynamicist from the National Physical Laboratory, as the first Principal.

As an apprentice at Portsmouth Royal Dockyard in 1909 Relf had gained a scholarship to the Royal College of Science and, following his appointment to the scientific staff of the National Physical Laboratory in 1912, had become Superintendent of the Aerodynamics Department in 1925. He had contributed numerous papers in the reports and memoranda of the Aeronautical Research Committee, the Philosophical Magazine, and aeronautical technical journals.

A popular story about Relf was that his real ambition in life was to become a great pianist, but that he had decided against a musical career after noticing that a large number of musicians starved. Instead he decided to earn his living as a scientist and to support his hobby with the benefit of a regular income. Certainly he was known as a concert-standard pianist, and the Chancellor remembers Relf as "an outstanding organ player".

Professor William Jolly Duncan (after whom Cranfield's Duncan Road is named) came from Hull University College to be Head of the Department of Aerodynamics. Soon afterwards as Registrar came Valentine Frederick ("Val") Knight, who during the war was Superintendent for Organisation at the Telecommunications Research Establishment, Britain's centre of radar development, at Malvern. P.R.R. ("Papa") Stocks followed as Bursar and Jack John Lynall as Chief Clerk.

Professor Robert Lickley, former chief project engineer of Hawker Aircraft, was appointed Head of the Department of Aircraft Design, but, says the first annual report, "great difficulty was experienced in finding suitable heads for the Departments of Aircraft Propulsion and Flight, and these appointments were not made until much later." The posts were eventually filled by Group Captain R.C. Hockey (Flight) and N.S. Muir (Propulsion). They were assisted by about twenty academic and related staff whose specialisations included production, materials, mathematics, electrical/electronics and aircraft systems.

Between his appointment and the opening day, Relf explained "the full story behind Cranfield's College of Aeronautics, believed to be the first national education centre devoted to aviation in the world". His medium was the *Bedfordshire Times & Standard* which, under the headline, COMMONWEALTH LOOKS TO CRANFIELD, rather breathlessly billed "an exclusive interview with the Principal, Mr Ernest Frederick Relf, CBE, ARCS, FRAeS, FRS".

This 'University of the Air', designed to produce to-morrow's leaders of industry and research in a sphere that is peculiarly British would draw to Bedfordshire some of the finest brains in the United Kingdom, the (sadly anonymous) interviewer forecast. "Through its doors may pass the Wilbur Wrights, the de Havillands and the Miles of to-morrow; men who will place the British Commonwealth in the forefront of aeronautical design, and prove to the world that Britain has the brains and the material to take a lead in the air in peace as in war."

The first of the two-year courses, to cover aerodynamics, aircraft design and propulsion, would commence in October, but - "Between now and that opening day, when a number of important figures are expected to attend the inaugural ceremony, a great deal of work has to be done. Buildings recently vacated by the RAF have to be converted into fully-equipped lecture-rooms and studies, vast quantities of equipment have to be unpacked from the crates which are arriving daily, aircraft must be purchased, lecturers engaged, and the would-be students themselves sorted out and interviewed."

We then come to Relf: "Soft-spoken Principal of the college that may change the whole history of British aviation, Mr Relf is equipped with a quiet, unassuming manner and a disarming smile that will cut through the stiffest regulations and energise the most lethargic governmental departments. Himself determined to have the college ready for its first flow of fifty students, he leaves the impression that having decided 'it shall be done', it will."

The *Times & Standard* explained the entry requirement thus: "Introducing a degree of elasticity hitherto unknown in British universities and colleges, there will be no demand for degrees or other evidence of examination successes from candidates wishing to take the course. Providing they have been educated to graduate standard, and can satisfy a competent board of examiners that they have the right stuff in them, applicants need fear no handicap through war-interrupted educations. Next autumn's course is, in fact, expected to contain a high proportion of ex-Service men."

Relf explained: "We want to provide a high-grade engineering, technical and scientific training in aeronautics to fit students for leadership in the aircraft industry, civil aviation, the Services, education, and research. We cannot do that if we turn away brilliant men because they suffer from examination nerves or gave up their studies to enter the Services."

Flying instruction, said the interviewer, would be given to those found medically fit, and experimental work taken out of the laboratory and the wind-tunnel, and taken into the air. Students would also "learn something of research methods by co-operating in staff research work".

Evidence of the world-wide interest aroused by the few brief announcements made at various times in Parliament could be seen in the number of applications already received - "many of them from the Dominions".

A "purely nominal" fee of £75 per year of four terms was being asked, while the cost of maintenance in the College Hall of Residence would amount to between £100 and £150 per year - "But it is hoped that large numbers of students will be sent to the College from aeronautical firms, and there can be little doubt that such scholarships will eventually be awarded."

Of Val Knight it was said: "His energetic efforts in preparing the ground since he arrived in January to find himself and his cause unknown have made him familiar to a large number of tradespeople in Bedford, for whose co-operation he and the Principal have expressed deep gratitude."

The interview then turned to the structure of Cranfield.

"The proposed two-year course, divided into three main departments, throws light upon the long and exhaustive training necessary before the modern aeronautical scientist may consider himself an expert in his subject. Research has travelled a long way since the hit-or-miss days of the century's early years, and no one who hopes to contribute to present aeronautical knowledge can avoid specialising.

"That specialisation will be introduced during the second year, when students have passed beyond the stage devoted to providing themselves with the broad common basis upon which to build. According to their individual needs, they will be guided into an exhaustive study of the three subjects into which aeronautical science naturally divides itself; aerodynamics, practical design, and aircraft propulsion. As will be seen these divisions each cover a vast field of inquiry, and it is necessary for the specialist to enjoy more than general knowledge of, say, aircraft propulsion before he can really get down to creative work.

"The Department of Aerodynamics will provide a basic understanding of fluid flow, which lies at the root of all aerodynamic phenomena, and from this will be built more detailed knowledge of aerodynamic behaviour in aircraft and component parts. Elaborating upon general principles underlying equilibrium and stability in flight, instruction will be given upon vital questions of manoeuvrability and control.

"High speeds are forcing upon designers a more careful investigation of compressibility effects occurring at speeds at and beyond the speed of sound. To-morrow's experts will be introduced to the problem during their second year, even though the subject is still one of the greatest controversy. Wind tunnel and flight tests will be performed so that students have direct contact with the practical significance of the lecture-room.

"Design and strength of aircraft structures will be discussed in the Department of Aircraft Design, where a training will be provided unobtainable elsewhere in the United Kingdom. Here the emphasis will be upon the application of results of theory to practical design of aircraft.

"Terrific loads are imposed upon an aircraft during manoeuvres, and a pound weight may increase to many times that amount in a tight turn. The strain imposed upon wing and fuselage structures will be studied in the laboratory, and pupils will discover experimentally whether or not the strength calculations made in the 'back-room' are borne out in practice.

'Gas-turbine and jet methods of propulsion are to-day popularly considered the only means of travel for the future, but there is no certainty that the reciprocating engine that served the warring nations with such marked success is as yet out-moded. While that is so, and because the jet-engine designer of to-morrow may still require knowledge of to-day's Merlins and Sabres, principles of design and operation of the reciprocating engine will be studied, although more weight given to the later discoveries."

Once trained by Cranfield and armed with its diploma, "the student will be guided as to his future career by the College careers advisory committee... A glance at the Board of Governors reveals that, in many cases, leaders of industry are included, and suggests that there will be little difficulty in finding a place for the fully qualified man. Indeed, it is more probable that the Empire's demands will exceed the supply, providing Britain and the Dominions enjoy some freedom of development in civil and military aviation."

The interview concluded: "After a period during which they have seen the greatest single contribution to the progress of man utilised as a weapon of destruction, it must be a source of satisfaction to Mr. Relf and the staff of Cranfield College of Aeronautics that they should be launched at last upon a job of creative education in the world of aviation."

As the interviewer had observed, there was still plenty to do before take-off. With both the ETPS and the College of Aeronautics sharing Cranfield at the beginning, the problems of accommodation had to be resolved, and an allocation of buildings was made at an Air Ministry meeting in February, 1946.

The Ministry also agreed to carry out all necessary modifications to the buildings, including converting two hangars into large laboratories by sub-dividing them with partitions, providing a flat roof and installing heating. Heavily-armoured doors were replaced with brick walls and plenty of windows.

The Airmen's Dining Hall (now named in honour of Stafford Cripps) became a Hall of Assembly, with a library, main lecture hall, two common rooms and a recreation room for teaching staff. The ground floors of barrack blocks were converted into small laboratories, with lecture rooms and drawing offices on the upper floors, and the first floor of the old RAF Headquarters Building was rearranged to provide offices for the Principal, Registrar, Bursar and clerical staff.

Lastly, the original Sergeants' Mess (renamed Mitchell Hall in 1948 in honour of R.J. Mitchell, of Spitfire fame) was converted into a Hall of Residence for the first-year intake of students, with a common room, dining and games rooms and running water in all study-bedrooms, and a bungalow was built adjoining the Hall as a house for the Steward.

"These arrangements", says the first Annual Report, "were sufficient to meet the first intake of students in October, 1946, but no more." So plans were made to build two more wings to the Hall of Residence for the next intake, and to provide more houses for senior staff.

"Planning was, indeed, carried a great deal further than this", the report adds, "and the architect was instructed to prepare comprehensive plans for the more distant future, on the assumption that by then the College would be the sole occupant of Cranfield."

These plans included additional wings to the Officers' Mess (later renamed after F.W. Lanchester) to accommodate some 300 students. But in December 1946 the Air Ministry decided that the EPTS should move from Cranfield much earlier than expected – by July the following year.

This would leave the College with more buildings in which to accommodate the next student entry in October, 1947, and the building plans were therefore "postponed for the time being."

Nevertheless, there was an urgent problem in providing married quarters for senior lecturers and other teaching and ancillary staff – a total, with clerical grades, mechanics, caterers, labourers and others, then amounting to some 220. "The lecturers", the report noted, "are very dissatisfied with the accommodation at present provided for them in the old airmen's married quarters."

Equipment, too, was a problem, but there were two Halifax bombers, a few Tiger Moths and four Ansons for instruction; and in the best traditions of military life, wind tunnels, laboratory and other essential materials were "scrounged", most notably a 3ft 6in diameter double flow wind tunnel and precision measuring machines "liberated" from Germany.

An extensive museum of World War Two aircraft was started, with a B-17, Liberator, prototype Lincoln, Tempest 2, Me163, FW190, Junkers 388 and a Vought Corsair.

The first report also looked closely at:

The students: "It had been generally agreed, after many authorities had been consulted, that the number of students in each entry for the two-year course should be about 50. After a prospectus had been printed and distributed in the Spring of 1946, and notices of the College course sent to the Press, a total of 106 applications were received from candidates for admission.

"The Principal and the Heads of Department constituted the Board of Entry which was to be responsible for selection. It had originally been intended to interview all applicants, but this proved to be physically impossible. Accordingly, some students were admitted and some were rejected on their paper qualifications, but all doubtful cases were interviewed.

"Eight students from the Royal Air Force and five from the Royal Navy were taken on the recommendation of their respective Services. The final list contained 49 names. Of these, two from India and one home applicant later failed to come, one left early owing to sickness, and one to take up an appointment.

"One further student joined after the commencement of the session, making the present number 45. Of these, six of the

Royal Air Force students have come for the first year only of the two-year course. About half the students are graduates, and of the remainder, most have obtained good results in the Higher National Certificate.

"On the whole, the average is not quite as good as had been hoped, and it was necessary to alter the teaching somewhat from the original conception of the syllabus, in order to meet the needs of the students. Nevertheless, the first intake is not unsatisfactory, and the best students are distinctly good."

The teaching: "The general principle has been followed of using the mornings for lectures and the afternoons for practical work in the laboratories and drawing offices. All the weekdays except Saturdays have been so employed.

"It was hoped to leave a few free periods for private study and reading, but the ground to be covered and the general level of knowledge of the students has so far not enabled this to be done. Saturday mornings have generally been free, except for a few special lectures, for example, in mathematics.

"Several general evening lectures on broad topics have been arranged and have been very successful. They were attended by students and staff, and officers of the Empire Test Pilots' School were also invited to come if they so decided."

Research: "It has not been found possible yet to inaugurate any experimental researches in the College, though a number of ideas for future activities are developing. Some of the staff have found time for original work of a theoretical nature, and the results have been incorporated in a series of College Reports. In one of them a student was the second author.

"All of them have been communicated to the appropriate bodies of the Aeronautical Research Council, and copies are being sent to any interested persons or outside organisations, often in exchange for their own research reports."

The future: "The second intake of students for the two-year course is now under consideration, and at the moment of writing the number of students already accepted approaches 40. The establishment of short courses has been investigated by obtaining the views of many in Industry, the Services and the Airline Operating Companies.

"The enquiry is still in progress, but a preliminary analysis of the results reveals little more than the great difficulty in making right decisions. The importance of extending the scope of College activities in this way is fully realised, and every endeavour will be made to arrive at an early solution of the problem."

Generally, though, everyone seemed quite happy with that first hectic year. "In spite of very considerable difficulties and delays in the early stages", the report concludes, "the College was opened on the appointed day, October 15,

1946, albeit with fewer facilities, especially in the laboratories, than had been hoped.

"Improvisation was necessary to meet this lack, but it cannot be said that there was any really serious interference with the proposed scheme of the teaching. The students found their task a hard one, especially at the beginning, but are settling into the routine of the work and are on the whole making satisfactory progress.

"There is every reason to be fairly satisfied with the first full year's work in building up the College, and there are signs that it will develop approximately on the broad lines defined by the Aeronautical Research Committee, the Fedden Report, and the subsequent policy discussions of the Board of Governors."

———

WHAT that report could not convey, of course, was the tremendous atmosphere at Cranfield in those early days. "There was a terrific esprit", recalls P.A. (Phil) Digger, who arrived there as an accounts clerk, "straight out of the RAF", in July 1947, and retired as General Secretary (and honorary graduate) in October, 1987.

"It was a great community, with wonderful cricket and rowing clubs, and at one stage the students had a vintage Rolls-Royce, called Matilda, which they used on sports outings, so that the Cranfield contingent always arrived in style.

"When the RAF moved out, their Officers' Mess became the second-year students' Hall of Residence, and when they moved in they didn't just move all their kit, but the engines which they kept in their rooms to work on."

Because Wharley End was then so remote, everyone had bikes to get anywhere beyond the perimeter roads, then unimaginatively named North, South, East and West Roads. And they also rode them in Lanchester Hall and staged cycle races along the corridors.

One popular, semi-official, annual event was the aeronautical students' rocket competition. It was all properly organised, with the students designing and building rockets and firing them off behind Lanchester Hall. As these inventions developed in engineering and in size (but not a long way in design beyond Bonfire Night technology) they grew to the stage at which students were firing off beer barrels on broomsticks. One year's output was so successful that a local newspaper carried reports of mysterious UFOs being sighted over Bedfordshire.

In addition to the liberated or reparation equipment from Germany, the students had access to Halifaxes, Ansons and Tiger Moths (one Halifax was re-conscripted for, and lost in, the Berlin airlift in 1948) and these provided fun as well as education.

Digger recalls the night when a group of students wheeled a bright yellow Halifax – called The Knocker, perhaps because of the noise it made – down to the village and parked it outside The Swan in Cranfield High Street.

Then, the story goes, they phoned the *Daily Express* and reported that a Halifax had made a forced landing, missing the runway and narrowly avoiding the houses in Cranfield village, but coming down in the High Street. When reporters phoned the landlord, he said "Nonsense!", but was asked to look out of his window.

"Good grief!" he said. "I didn't hear that thing coming down in the night." But by the time the reporters and cameramen arrived, the Halifax had just as mysteriously disappeared – wheeled back to the College by the students.

"Another time they wheeled a Fleet Air Arm plane, with foldaway wings, down the street", says Digger, "and they once removed a window from the lounge of Lanchester Hall, lifted a student's car from the car-park, parked it inside, and put the window back. They worked hard, but they certainly knew how to have fun, too."

In fact the students had realised, fairly early on, that they were working too hard. The intention had been to turn out aeronautical engineers well-rounded in all aspects of the industry and capable of assuming leading roles in it. All students were required to study Design, Propulsion, Aerodynamics and Production, with one subject as a major interest, but nevertheless with a high degree of proficiency in all the others.

During the second year the students realised that they were being asked to do too much, and staged a short strike.

Professor David Keith-Lucas, former Professor of Aeronautics, said: "They were however a hand-picked bunch and pretty bright. To a great extent therefore the object of producing leaders in the aircraft industry was achieved; quite a few of those early generations became Chief Designers, Chief Engineers, even Managing Directors and Air Marshals, not to mention Professors."

———

ONE OF THE first and most distinguished recruits to the College of Aeronautics was Wing Commander Charles McClure, AFC, who had done invaluable work as a Wartime test pilot on Spitfires and Hurricanes.

McClure, educated at Winchester and Trinity College, Oxford (where he read modern greats, rowed in the Head of the River crew and learned to fly with the University Air Squadron) started his career at the De Havilland Technical School.

He built and flew his own "Flying Flea", an early type of micro-light, was commissioned into the Reserve of Air Force Officers and in 1938 joined the RAF Volunteer Reserve. After initial service as a ferry pilot, he was sent as a test pilot to the Royal Aircraft Establishment at Farnborough.

There he and his comrades risked their lives helping scientists remedy worrying faults in the Spitfires and Hurricanes, and McClure was later involved in testing Britain's first jet, the Gloster E28/39, the "Gloster Whittle".

Awarded the AFC for his wartime work at Farnborough, he had a brief posting to the Empire Test Pilots' School and returned there in 1945 as chief test pilot, evaluator of captured aircraft, and Wing Commander Flying. Then, after leaving the RAF and working for a short time at the Ministry of Civil Aviation, he joined Cranfield in 1947.

McClure, who was appointed Professor of Flight in 1973 and retired in 1978, died in September, 1994, at the age of 78, when *The Times* recalled, in a fulsome obituary, his achievements at Cranfield:

"He set up a department of flight and initiated a programme of research and testing for outside firms which produced valuable income for Cranfield. With some of this money he bought three early Jetstream aircraft (a design with engines from Turbomeca which had to that point made little impact on the civil aviation world).

"Seeing the potential of the Jetstream, McClure persuaded Turbomeca to improve its service to customers and the reliability of its engines. He always claimed that without this friendly persuasion, the Jetstream would never have been taken up by Scottish Aviation and become the export success it now is.

"McClure sold one of the Jetstreams for twice the price he had originally paid for all three, and the other two are still in the service of the university".

———

ANOTHER fascinating glimpse into the history of Cranfield came when the College of Aeronautics celebrated its 40th anniversary and John Spillman, Professor of Aerodynamics, remembered the early days:

"The table mats stopped flying and the 50 students, all in jackets and ties, who were seated at the long table, rose as the members of staff entered and made their way to the top table at the far end of the dining room. Yet another 'dining in' night was starting! However, things were better now, only once a week instead of every night except Friday, as it was in the first term."

A keen observer in 1947 would have noticed that the average age of the students was about 28 [as, indeed, it has remained] and that of the staff was fewer than ten years more. This small age difference and the fact that everyone lived on campus made the relationship between staff and students a close collaboration in what all recognised as a pioneering activity, the first year of the College of Aeronautics.

"It was the keenness of all concerned to make a success of the venture that overcame the difficulties of having few major experimental facilities, no aircraft in which to fly and being almost intruders at RAF Cranfield, home of the Empire Test Pilots School," said Spillman. In the first year, all students took lectures and laboratories in the four main departments, Aerodynamics, Design, Flight and Propulsion, as well as in the subsidiary ones such as Electronics and Materials.

"One laboratory [in Materials] will be remembered by everyone there. Each student had to cast small ingots of a variety of metal alloys and subsequently test them to destruction by putting them in a vice and hitting them with a big hammer. This caused so much hilarity and confusion as students missed or pieces of metal flew everywhere that it was the subject of a cartoon as well as the basis of a sketch in the regular staff-student socials held each mid-term.

"On these occasions, the whole campus population met for a get-together and the students put on a series of almost impromptu sketches and songs which expressed in a light-hearted way their feelings of how things were going. One got the impression that the members of staff who were the subjects of the fun felt it a compliment to be chosen, and on occasions potential problems aired in this way were avoided without rancour."

Spillman recalled the arrival of the Avro Ansons, the flying classrooms of those early days, being greeted with tremendous enthusiasm, which only waned slightly in the poor student elected to wind up the undercarriage by hand. Students had to wear parachute harness in the aircraft although the parachutes themselves were stored at the back of the cabin; fortunately, they were never put to the test.

"Surprisingly, the flight test programme was very similar to that of today, from position error corrections to stick forces and movements per 'g'. It is an interesting thought that the 40 years since then is almost half the time since the first powered flight.

"It seems strange to realise that transonic and supersonic aerodynamics were in their infancy in those days and that re-inforced plastics were unknown as structural materials, yet the advantages of laminar boundary layer flow and the difficulties of achieving it were appreciated."

As was to remain the case, all students studying Aeronautics had the opportunity to pilot aircraft, but relatively few had the time to qualify for a private pilot's licence. After about six hours' dual in a Tiger Moth, one was sent solo, said Spillman – "usually after undergoing the alarming experience of instruction in getting out of a spin.

"When Bert Russell got out of the front cockpit the centre of gravity moved rearwards significantly and many a student had a nose soaring experience on attempting his first solo landing. Bert loved mushrooms, and often a student had unscheduled instruction in low-level flying when he searched the airfield for them!"

All students lived in Hall and in spite of food rationing enjoyed not only three cooked meals a day but additional sandwiches in the evening. These were served in the bar, so the routine after dinner at 1800 hours was to work in the study rooms until about 2100 hours, go for a game of squash and a shower, followed by sandwiches and drinks in the bar then a return to work at about 2230 hours until 0200 or later. Students worked to the sound of Midnight From Munich, the US Forces programme, which would puncture the air until the early hours. Not surprisingly, there were many bleary-eyed students going in for breakfast at 0855 the next day.

Like Phil Digger's, Spillman's recollection is that the students worked hard, but – "occasionally there would be an outburst and everyone would take the evening off. On one such occasion the Warden panicked at the noise and high spirits and sent for the fire brigade – quite unnecessary of course."

There were very few cars on campus in those days and a favourite relaxation was to walk across the airfield to the village to either the Rex cinema or enjoy 'the works' (eggs, bacon, beans, bangers and chips) at a 'cafe' in one of the houses. The average body weight of that first student intake is not recorded, however - "Sports activities were popular, but the small number of students often meant that some had to play in the squash team immediately after an away game of hockey or soccer. After the squash team had been trounced 5-0 by the men's team of the Bedford Squash Club, they challenged the ladies' team – with the same result, but a more enjoyable social occasion afterwards!"

Spillman says that both staff and students were very conscious of being in at the beginning of something new and exciting. A great deal of time was spent discussing the constitution of the Students' Society and the Senior Common Room. Distinguished visitors were many, and frequent, and enthusiasm for the new venture was tremendous.

"One often heard the phrase that the College of Aeronautics was training 'leaders of industry', possibly first voiced by Sir Harold Roxbee Cox, or Sir Roy Fedden, who often spent an evening talking informally with the students.

"Certainly all were aware that great things were expected of them, and they accepted the challenge eagerly. When I look now and see what they achieved in industry and the services and how Cranfield has grown and prospered, I see their success."

———

ONE of those earliest entrants, described in the student magazine of March 1949 as a Tchaikovsky-loving cross-country runner, was Tom Corkill, who at the time of the 40th anniversary was Training Manager for British

Aerospace at Stevenage. Recalling those early days, he asked:

"What happens if you combine the best available teachers, the most advanced facilities and equipment, and a varied, even motley, collection of enthusiastic would-be aeronautical engineers and enforce with great kindness, but firmness, a strict regime of hard demanding work at high pressure?

"I believe I know the answer, for I was there, not quite at the very start of the Cranfield epoch, but two years later. In 1946, so the first brochure of all said, the College of Aeronautics opened its doors 'to provide a high grade engineering, technical and scientific training in aeronautics to fit students for leadership'.

"Since then, Cranfield is still recognisable for its excellence in teaching and research, but otherwise grown beyond imaginings in its scope.

"The most important gift in my opinion that Cranfield bestowed is almost metaphysical, but not quite, and there is the belief that most things are possible and the 'yes' and 'why not?' are preferable expressions to others which convey doubt, hesitation, or fear of the unknown.

"This gift goes with others: the urge to create and improve and to want to grasp opportunities. I suppose that I cannot claim with absolute accuracy that Cranfield alone gave rise to these attitudes – but I certainly felt them within myself and, what is more, there is a remarkable correlation between them and the actions of many of my ex-Cranfield colleagues.

"How did Cranfield do this? I believe it was by following measured doses of theory with violent and concentrated practice – such as being confronted suddenly with a noisy, hot jet-engine or rocket motor to operate and then evaluate – or having to make sense of flight-test results from one's own measurements in a genuine flying aircraft and, through research, gaining confidence to argue on (almost!) equal terms with tutors and, above all, to feel free of the tramlines and curbs that marked the work of the first degree."

Tom Corkill then posed a second question: what else has Cranfield given to British Aerospace? His reply: "It has given people, and in abundance. It is difficult to be precise as to how many people came to British Aerospace and its predecessor companies since the beginning, but it is at least 160, included within which have been many notables.

"At the present time [1986] there are two Divisional Managing Directors who 'trained' (the first brochure's word) at Cranfield, John Parkhouse at the Army Weapons Division and Sidney Gillibrand at the Civil Aircraft Division.

"And I cannot resist mentioning two others I admire greatly: John Fozard, who did so much in designing and developing the Harrier, and Mark Dowden, who set in motion the Research and New Projects work in Guided Weapons that led directly to our most prolific of all systems, the 'Rapier'.

"Such a rich outpouring of talent justifies and crowns the imaginative philosophy that became a reality at Cranfield."

———

TO TRANSFORM the philosophy into reality, though, often meant the new College would face stormy times caused by sea changes in Britain's political and economic climate – not least in those very early days as its development was limited by the severe austerity of the 1940s.

Even so, early developments included the setting up of a fifth department, of Aircraft Economics and Production, and with the appointment of the first research assistants, recognition that the College would have to introduce a successful Research and Development programme to attract commercial sponsorship and funding to supplement its Government grant.

In December 1948 the need for a rigorous approach to planning was recognised when a new administrative body, the Senate, was established to assist the Principal. It was made up of Heads of Department, with the Principal as Chairman and the Registrar as Secretary.

This new Senate, with, "subject to the overriding control of the Governors, responsibility for the entire superintendence, control and management of the College and its affairs," was followed in June 1950 with the

Governors' approval of new Statutes, defining College organisation, administration and financial policy.

By March 1951, says archivist John Harrington, there was evidence of pressure beginning to build on the College and the onset of a period of crisis and instability which seemed to threaten its future:

"The pressures, constraints and challenges imposed on the College in the period between 1951-55 are essentially the same as those facing higher education today – the need to seek ways to bring in additional revenue, through the promotion of commercial activities, in order to supplement public money and to demonstrate to the funding authority value for money in terms of the quantity and quality of productivity and output."

For the governors and staff at this time, this pressure manifested itself essentially in the need to reduce the College's costs per student. It also, for the first time, highlighted a debate that was to occupy much of the College's efforts up until receiving its Charter in 1969 – the need to move from its original aeronautical interest into a greater diversity of areas for teaching and research.

The concerns of those times are clear in the 1950-51 annual report: "During the year under review both the Governors and Staff were very conscious of the need to make the widest and most economic use of the exceptional equipment and facilities available at Cranfield.

"Much consideration has also been given to the possibility of widening the scope of the College and the Departments, and to the extent and direction of such developments.

"The main objects which the Governors had in mind... were first of all to extend the services which the College as a national institution could render the nation, secondly to utilise to better advantage the considerable quantity of apparatus and equipment available at the College, and thirdly to reduce the cost per student by increasing their number."

They were troubled times for Britain, too. A series of Sterling crises, devaluation, fears over Britain's balance of payments and the outbreak of war in Korea increased the economic pressure on Clement Atlee's Government (in which Sir Stafford Cripps still served), and the General Elections of 1950 and 1951 saw first a massive reduction in the Government's majority and then its defeat by the Conservatives under Sir Winston Churchill.

(Students took a lively interest: "At one General Election," Digger remembers, "they wrote VOTE CONSERVATIVE in huge letters on the roof of Number Two Hangar").

It was during this uncertain period that the College's first Principal, Ernest Relf, retired, and was succeeded in September 1951, to the surprise of some, by Air Vice-Marshal Sir Victor Goddard. To him came the same problems as before – the cost per student, finance for accommodation to handle larger student numbers, and

*Air Vice-Marshall
Sir Victor Goddard*

more money to attract the right students and staff for diversification into a wider range of activities.

The problem of attracting staff with the appropriate level of qualifications and experience was hindered by a serious discrepancy between the salaries of the College's academic staff and their University colleagues, because of Government-imposed restrictions on the salaries of civil servants and those with related pay.

There were also increased demands for high-calibre staff in industry, whose salary scales could not be matched by the College. But it would take many years of negotiations before the Ministry of Education recognised the Governors' request for academic salaries at the College to be brought into line with those of the universities.

Victor Goddard also faced the problem that had bedevilled Cranfield from the start – that of accommodation. His predecessor had been unable to get an increase in the grant-in-aid to finance the much-needed building of staff and student accommodation, particularly the much-delayed extension to Lanchester Hall.

The cost, plus a shortage of materials because of post-war industrial and housing building programmes, effectively ensured that Cranfield had to make do with the buildings it had inherited from the RAF at the beginning. This difficult situation actually increased costs, because buildings which, for defence reasons, had been widely dispersed over a large area, were more expensive to maintain.

Added to this was the cost of maintaining and servicing the large airfield, and Goddard wanted to revise accounting procedures to show the cost of the airfield and its building separately from the costs of the College's academic activities.

The cost implications caused by lack of adequate staff housing was noted in the annual report for 1952-53: "This shortage incurs the continuous expense of transport to convey staff to the College from the surrounding countryside, which is peculiarly lacking in public transport, and emphasises further the need for adequate financial provision for capital works."

Victor Goddard had made his own transport arrangements: "He had a penchant for showmanship," remembers Digger, "and when he saw a huge American limousine being advertised in a newspaper, he decided the College should buy it as the Principal's car."

Not everyone appreciated its grandeur, however. Goddard sent it to Bedford station one day to collect Sir Frederick Handley Page, who was paying an official visit. Handley Page flatly refused to enter the vehicle. He said: 'Cranfield is a British institution, and I'm not going to arrive at it in an American car!"

Goddard, meanwhile, struggled on with the same old problems, like increasing students numbers – although even if it could accommodate them, Cranfield appears to be have been having difficulty attracting sufficient candidates of the right calibre. And the potential ending of National Service, which had acted as a stimulus in persuading students into post-graduate education, only exacerbated the situation.

The 1950-51 report, recognising the need to achieve maximum use of the College's resources, has a sly swipe at the Government's lack of support for technical education: "In the lack of any precise or even general direction from above," the report declares, "it remains a subject which, while pregnant with possibilities, does not readily lend itself to any immediate practical solution.

"The need for further development of technical education throughout the country is now generally realised and has been under consideration for some time at high level. Bearing this in mind, we at Cranfield feel the need for some indication as to the part which Cranfield should take in any development of this kind, and particularly how Cranfield, with its superb technical equipment and other potentialities, can best fit into a national scheme."

In 1952-53 came the worst of the crisis. First the Ministry of Education, at a request from the Treasury, forced the Governors to accept an independent review of the College's organisation and work. Then Cranfield had to go back to the Ministry for a supplement to its grant-in-aid before the end of the year.

Several strategies were agreed to solve Cranfield's problems, including a well-planned publicity campaign to raise the College's public profile and win support. A series of articles about its work appeared in the technical Press, and a radio and television programme helped spread the message.

But the biggest coup of all was a visit by the Duke of Edinburgh – the first of several by the Duke, who became the official Visitor of the Cranfield Institute of Technology following its inauguration in May, 1970.

His first visit, in October 1952, was seen by Goddard as very important for Cranfield as it tried to establish its academic identity, and he told Heads of Department in a memo shortly before the occasion: "It is not only a great honour to this College to be receiving a visit by the Duke of Edinburgh, it is also a great opportunity, for his Royal Highness has become the leading patron of Technology.

"For the visit to be a success, it is necessary that The Duke of Edinburgh should take away very lively impressions of the potentialities of the people of this College as well as its equipment. What is said by His Royal Highness to those whose influence can aid or impede the future of this College is vitally important."

Success it was: the Duke, arriving at 11am, visited the Departments of Aerodynamics, Aircraft Design, Aircraft Propulsion, Flight, Aircraft Economics and Production as well as Lanchester Hall and the Library. He stayed until 4.30pm.

During his visit, it was noted with satisfaction, "The Duke displayed his well-known interest and knowledge of technological education... this, and many other visits, demonstrated the College's growing importance in the educational system of the country and to the aircraft industry."

Even so, Cranfield's survival depended on increasing student numbers and developing teaching and research activities in new areas to attract commercial sponsorship, and the annual report for the year ending March 1952 asked:

The Duke of Edinburgh, first 'patron of technology'

"Should the College confine itself solely to research and teaching of aeronautical or near aeronautical subjects? If not, what other subjects can suitably be taught at Cranfield... it is desirable for the happiness and health of Cranfield as a whole that the community should be increased in size and broadened in interest."

That was perhaps the first unequivocal statement in support of diversification, which was to become a Cranfield hallmark. Certainly there was much disappointment at Cranfield that although individual aircraft companies were sponsoring some students and funding commercial work, the College itself had failed to attract enough financial support from the aircraft industry as a whole in order to be able to reduce its dependence on the Government's grant-in-aid.

The need to offer a wider range of activities was further emphasised by the announcement by local authorities that they intended to cease the provision of grants to students for post-graduate education.

In 1954-55 the percentage of students at Cranfield supported by Local Education Authorities dropped from an average of 32 per cent in previous years to 23 per cent, and in November 1956 these grants were withdrawn entirely. The effect of this was to cause the College to seek further increases in the grant-in-aid to provide additional studentships for would-be applicants.

One ambitious innovation had been the beginning, in January 1953, of a Work Study School funded by industrial sponsors including ICI, Hoover and the British Institute of Management. The School, a significant step on the path to diversification, would evolve into one of the activities which combined to produce the prestigious Cranfield School of Management at the end of the 1960s.

Meanwhile management at Cranfield itself was experiencing some changes. In October 1952 the Principal had become directly responsible to the Governors, with the Senate retained solely as an advisory body. Then in June 1953, the first Chairman of the Board of Governors, Ludlow-Hewitt, resigned and was replaced by Sir Frederick Handley Page.

The constitution of the Board of Governors was altered to allow the appointment of additional committees and three

Deputy Chairmen who, with Handley Page, were effectively to lead the decision-making process.

Professor Denis Howe, chairman of the College of Aeronautics from 1986 to 1990, described Goddard as "a man with far-seeing ideas..." without "the experience to be able to implement them in an academic environment". Within three years of his appointment Goddard resigned as Principal and after a brief inter-regnum was succeeded in October 1955 by Professor Alfred Murphy, a distinguished metallurgist. To him would fall the task of steering Cranfield towards university status.

———

VICTOR GODDARD'S time as Principal brings back a fund of stories. "He was a very authoritarian man," says Phil Digger, "and the students over-reacted to him fairly frequently. You'd often hear the phrase 'He's acting the old Air Marshal again'.

"Goddard never gave people advice or made requests. He only gave orders, and one of them was that residents must not hang out washing on lines on Sundays. Well, that was obviously a mistake, because when he went to look out on his perfectly-manicured lawn the next Sunday morning, there was a washing-line from which was suspended a massive pair of extra-outsize ladies' bloomers!"

Another memorable incident occurred shortly before the Coronation. An enormous heavy wooden flagpole was somehow lifted from its position outside the administrative block, carried to Cayley Lodge, the former Commanding Officer's residence in which Goddard lived, and manhandled into position across both his front door and garage.

When Goddard arrived home, he couldn't get in to the house. He drove round to Lanchester Hall, found a bunch of students and asked, politely: "Someone has left some spare timber outside Cayley Lodge. I wonder whether a few of you gentlemen would give me a hand in removing it?" And, of course, they did.

Yet another Goddard story concerns Sir George Cayley himself, the man hailed by many as the father of aerodynamics who, in 1853, had a coachman fly across a valley at Brompton Hall near Scarborough in a glider he had designed. ("I was hired to drive, not to fly," the disgruntled servant said when he got out, and promptly handed in his notice).

Goddard deemed it appropriate to install a statue of Cayley in the entrance to the Stafford Cripps building. Some of the students found a statue of Venus and positioned it alongside. Then they put a couple of pennies into Cayley's outstretched hand, so it looked as though he was offering her money.

There was great enterprise shown in those days, too. "Once," remembers Digger, "the Royal Canadian Air Force, based in Renfrew, was updating its equipment and had a spare fighter plane, complete with armaments and its residual fuel – which was actually more fuel than we had in store in Cranfield.

Coronation Eve

at Goddard's

residence.

"The College said we'd like to buy it, and the Canadians asked for a nominal payment of one Canadian dollar, lunch for the pilot who was to fly it down and his return train fare to Scotland. Well, the second two were no problem, but because of currency exchange rules and paperwork we had terrible trouble getting that one Canadian dollar. We succeeded eventually, of course, and Cranfield got a great bargain.

"Yet another interesting aircraft Cranfield acquired was a Saunders-Roe jet-propelled flying-boat, SAR-01. We played around with it for a while and eventually took out the engine and gave it to Donald Campbell for Bluebird.

"We also bought a Liberator which had more or less only flown from the United States and little more and had only 50 hours on the clock. We bought that for just £50, and when it became surplus to requirements sold it as scrap – for £1,500."

It was Cranfield enterprise in action.

(opposite page)

Harmless fun? Cayley meets Venus in Stafford

Cripps

THE NEW team of Professor Murphy as Principal and Handley Page as Chairman of the Governors came with an upturn not only in Britain's economic situation but also in Cranfield's.

Alfred Murphy

In 1957, following a series of talks that had started with the Ministry of Works in 1951, the College at last assumed responsibility for the management of the Cranfield site, and in 1963 the freehold of the property including the airfield was transferred by deed from the Secretary of State for Air to the College.

That transfer of land and buildings would give some insurance against financial hardship in the years to come, while Cranfield pressed ahead with its chosen policy of diversification: new Departments of Aircraft Electrical Engineering and of Mathematics had been created in 1955, and a Department of Aircraft Materials in October, 1958.

But in 1957 there was a bombshell with the publication of the Government's infamous White Paper on Defence Policy. The Chancellor recalls: "It said, in effect, that we wouldn't want any pilots or aeronautics in future; it would all depend on unmanned missiles.

"It didn't quite put it like that, but the White Paper was a massive shock to us and the whole aircraft industry. It meant a different kind of Air Force, and it was a very disturbing report, and an idiotic one really.

"But it served as a warning that to us that the future of aeronautics was not going to be as rosy as we had previously thought, and that we had better find some means of diversifying."

The industry that had meant so much to the nation during the war, and had such high potential during the first years of peace now seemed, in the eyes of politicians at least, to have a fairly restricted future in Britain. One immediate effect was to start what was to become known as the Brain Drain, with the cream of Cranfield students heading to the USA for top jobs in their highly regarded aeronautics industry. Other technologies were also evolving and the emphasis moved away from advanced technology and towards a discipline of finding ways to save money. Production Engineering and Management became the key words.

This greater urgency to diversify meant that in 1958-60 an amendment to the Deed of Trust on which the College was founded was implemented to broaden its terms and allow Cranfield to engage in a wider range of activities.

New courses for application outside aeronautics were introduced alongside production and management, covering subjects such as fluid mechanics, control engineering and automotive engineering. The titles of three Departments were changed, in October 1961, to drop the word "Aircraft." So the Department of Aircraft Economics and Production became the Department of Production and Industrial Administration, and the Department of Aircraft Materials was cut to just the Department of Materials. Later, Management was to evolve into the Cranfield School of Management, and Propulsion declared that it was not solely concerned with

*Sir Harold
Roxbee Cox*

aeronautics and developed into a new School of Mechanical Engineering.

In a Handley Page lecture at Cranfield, Professor Keith-Lucas recalled: "The time came when students studying, say, welding technology in the Department of Materials no longer wanted a qualification with an aeronautical flavour and the very name, College of Aeronautics, was regarded as a disincentive to growth."

At this crucial stage of Cranfield's career, Frederick Handley Page, one of its greatest champions, died in April, 1962. But continuity was assured in August by the appointment as his successor as Chairman another who had been there from the start, Sir Harold Roxbee Cox.

Early the following year the Ministry of Education's Cost Investigation Unit made a detailed investigation of the College's finance and organisation and called for economies, ready for the replacement of the grant-in-aid by a new Direct Grant in 1963-64.

This, though, was the time of a national review of higher education being conducted by a Committee of Inquiry under Lord Robbins, whose recommendations were expected to determine the shape of higher education, and with it the future of Cranfield, for years ahead.

Evidence submitted to the Robbins Committee by the College was intended to substantiate its claim for recognition of its status as the nucleus of a new post-graduate Institute of Technology. And the Committee reported favourably on many aspects of the College's work.

Staff were encouraged that Robbins appeared to show Cranfield's staff-student ratio, for which it had been repeatedly criticised, as comparable with current university post-graduate courses, and that its costs were not inconsistent with others for post-graduate teaching and research.

But the Robbins Report, published in October, 1963, concluded; "We are not happy that a relatively small college of this kind should have the power to award its own degrees. We recommend, therefore, that if the College remains at about its present size and wishes its students to be eligible for higher degree, it should be urged to form an appropriate association with a university."

It also recommended that Cranfield be brought within the same funding arrangements as the universities – under the University Grants Committee.

So, soon after the Government signalled its acceptance of the Robbins Report with the White Paper on Higher Education in November, 1963, the UGC, in consultation with College authorities, established an Academic Advisory Committee to make specific recommendations for Cranfield's future development.

Its main conclusions, noted in the 1963-64 annual report, were that "the strength of the College and its associated institutions lay in their specialised experience of teaching at post-graduate and post-experience level, and in their exceptional facilities for experimental research, and that their best contribution to the national technological effort would be to develop as an exclusively or mainly post-graduate institution providing courses in engineering science, technology and management subjects directly related to the needs of industry."

Although that statement encapsulates the essential characteristics of what was to become the Cranfield Institute of Technology, it was to take six years of negotiation with the Secretary of State for Education before that dream could be realised.

In the meantime the Ministry tried to pressure Cranfield into accepting affiliation with some existing university, such as Birmingham, or with the Council for National Academic Awards, the body empowered to award degrees to students at the new polytechnics.

But in July, 1967, the College presented Her Majesty The Queen with a Petition for the Grant of a Royal Charter, along with a draft charter for a new institution to be called The Cranfield Institute of Technology.

Its aims: to advance, disseminate and apply learning and knowledge in the disciplines of the sciences, engineering, technology and management (and) to promote and encourage the application of that knowledge and learning to the practices of design, development and manufacture and to the organisation of industry and the public services.

———

ALL these developments, especially the drift away from aeronautics, were watched with less than enthusiasm by a man for whom they meant the abandonment of a dream – Sir Roy Fedden. His views come over loud and clear in *By Jupiter: the life of Sir Roy Fedden* by Bill Gunston. He writes: "In the post-graduate field, Cranfield was from the start the tangible model of Fedden's ideals.

"He had never comprehended the ways of the British academic. Not having been to a university himself, he was astonished that his brother Romilly should have taken his bath at Cambridge in a large tin container brought into his room by his bedder, and filled and emptied by the said servant using a bucket.

"Not having suffered a career amongst professors, he was likewise astonished that they should themselves construct balances for their wind-tunnels, making their own gears and filing the teeth by hand. Against such a background the revolution of Cranfield can be seen in perspective.

"Like MIT and Gottingen, the new centre of advanced technology was to have the most complete and most advanced equipment that could be found. Such excellent tools were, thought Fedden, generally regarded by the academics as un-British and rather degrading. The national tradition was to be so superior that better results could be obtained with bits of string and sealing wax."

Once established, however, Cranfield was able to carve out its own enormous niche in the world of advanced technology without too many academics looking down their noses at its fine equipment, he says.

"Until about 1960 its work was directed entirely towards the broad field of aerospace, its central role being to turn out previously qualified aeronautical engineers with the additional letters DCAe after their names. These letters soon came to be appreciated all over the world, especially in the United States, where a man with the College of Aeronautics Diploma could choose his employer and almost choose his salary.

"But Cranfield increasingly wanted the power to award not just a diploma but a degree, such as an MSc or DEng, having immediate and universal recognition."

Then in April 1957, says Gunston, almost echoing the words of the Chancellor, came the "incredible" White Paper on Defence in which was expressed the belief that the RAF would be 'unlikely to require' any new designs or fighters or bombers but would instead arm itself with guided missiles.

This "nonsensical" edict threw the aircraft industry into turmoil, drastically cut the entry to Cranfield, and made the College ponder on diversification.

"Such a move was expressly contrary to the ideals of Cripps, as vociferously expressed by his 'disciple' Fedden, who remained a Governor. To Fedden the vital ingredient needed for Cranfield to fulfil its purpose was its devotion to aerospace."

If it became diversified, thought Fedden, "you could have the most marvellous structures department in the world, attracting structural engineers from all industries; but if the leadership is not centred in doing the impossible – as aviation has had to do throughout its history – the vital spark will be lost, and there will be nothing to stop Cranfield degenerating into just another institute of technology."

The debate continued. Then in 1961 the Government set up the Robbins Committee on Higher Education to examine and to reshape the whole field of higher education in Britain.

According to Gunston, Fedden noted with gloom that "The average age of the Committee is about 60, its constitution is almost entirely academic, and there are no representatives from the modern precision engineering industry, or from any organisations familiar with the types of people needed in the coming generations to govern the country, to build up and manage industry progressively, and deal with the tremendous competition from all over the world".

Fedden was not alone in being apprehensive: so was everyone else who knew anything about British industry.

In November 1963 the Robbins Committee's findings were at last published. Fedden commented: "I feel like Job: the thing I greatly feared hath come upon me!"

He was appalled that the Committee recommended Cranfield be brought within the ambit of the University Grants Committee; that it did not like the idea of "a relatively small college of this kind" having power to award its own degrees, and suggested it should be urged to form an appropriate association with a university.

Fedden carefully read the entire report. He then commented that he understood exactly how, given the available data, the back-room civil servants who had written the report had arrived at their conclusions.

"He regarded them as extremely serious and well-intentioned," writes Gunston, "but, because of the complete ignorance on the part of the Committee and the civil servants of the nation's needs in advanced technology, correct conclusions were impossible.

"Robbins appeared to think size was everything, and to want to turn out vast numbers of average-quality engineers. What the nation needed with increasing urgency were the 'Flag Officer' breed – no matter in what small numbers – who had knowledge, vision, and character for leadership. Robbins he regarded as an unmitigated disaster.

Cranfield's Senate had issued a paper reviewing the Robbins recommendations, meekly falling into line with them, and saying nothing about aerospace but plenty about diversification and size.

Fedden called the paper "weak and indeterminate... I have heard all I want to, for some time, about diversification... I am not mesmerised by size. If we realise our goal of quality and only turn out 75 students a year we should make our awards on our own and not be beholden to anyone..."

There followed a long period of extraordinary strain and uncertainty, which often at times assumed a personal nature as those involved split into cliques, lobbied behind the scenes, and at times almost appeared to lose sight of what the nation most urgently needed through the intensity of the internecine conflict.

Writes Gunston: "Whereas in Fedden's immediate post-Robbins documents one found 'tooth and nail' quite often, the recurring phrase in 1964 and 1965 seemed to be 'a thread of misinterpretation'. Fedden's own answer was for Cranfield to settle at a size not greatly in excess of 1,000 students and to be called The Royal College of Aerospace (degree-awarding, of course), with 'logical and analogous' satellites such as The School of International Transport and Communications."

By 1966, after long deliberations by an Academic Advisory Committee appointed by the University Grants Committee, Fedden proposed a small committee formed from members of the Cranfield Society and the Royal Aeronautical Society to look at the problem.

"Wires got crossed, perfectly plain statements were interpreted in unexpected ways, and old friendships became strained. But it all came right – more or less – in the end.

"Cranfield received a Royal Charter, changed its name to The Cranfield Institute of Technology, yet for a while contrived to seek the elusive ideals true to the spirit of quality laid down by Cripps and Fedden. Only after Fedden's death did what is now called the CIT take a wrong turning.

The Royal Charter for

Cranfield Institute of

Technology

"Cranfield afflicted by Robbins could have tried to shut itself in an ivory tower, and it might conceivably have withered away there; but while Fedden lived this would have been impossible."

THE NEW Cranfield Institute of Technology formally achieved University status on December 31, 1969 with Professor Murphy as its first Vice-Chancellor. Lord Kings Norton, the immediate past Chairman of Governors, became its first Chancellor, and after only one day in office, on New Year's Day 1970, Professor Murphy's successor as Vice-Chancellor was named as Dr Henry Chilver. CIT, as it was inevitably to become known, was ceremonially inaugurated on May 8, 1970, with the announcement that

Dr Henry
Chilver

the Queen had appointed The Duke of Edinburgh as its Visitor.

The Chilver years, lasting until 1989, are seen as pivotal in Cranfield's development. His *Who's Who* entry chronicles the passage of a research engineer through the academic hierarchy (Bristol, Cambridge and University College, London) to university administration, the public sector – he was chairman of the Post Office, 1980-81 – and ultimately to industry and commerce. Along the way he picked up a knighthood, a life peerage, a fellowship of the Royal Society – for, among other things, his research into the stability of structures – five honorary degrees and a clutch of chairmanships including those of the Milton Keynes Development Corporation and the Interim Committee on Teachers' Pay.

One view of the man, his work and his philosophy appeared in a profile written in *The Independent* to coincide with his appointment as chairman of the Universities Funding Council in 1989.

It declared: "Henry Chilver, out-going Vice-Chancellor of Cranfield Institute of Technology, describes himself as 'a radical Tory'. He is widely reputed to have the ear of the Prime Minister" [then Mrs Margaret Thatcher].

Within the universities, opinions about Lord Chilver varied: 'There are few public figures of whom one knows so little', one academic comments. 'He is forever questioning (one)... in a terribly pretentious way about the meaning of life and things like that', another says.

"To some he is very good at drawing out young talent, for others he is an ideas man, and to a third group he is 'a safe pair of hands' to be relied upon by governments of whatever political complexion. (His knighthood came on the recommendation of a Labour government, his peerage through the Tories). 'He is a relatively flexible person', another observer says. 'He likes the corridors of power'.

"A former colleague says that, in the late 1960s, when Lord Chilver was director of the Centre for Environmental Studies, his politics were hard to discern, but today he is committed to 'fairly crude market solutions'."

The Independent went on: "Lord Chilver has said that universal knowledge can lead to universal wealth, and that parts of the university system are decaying because they have lost contact with the real world... Perhaps Cranfield is a model for the realism and relevance Lord Chilver has in mind...

"At Cranfield, Lord Chilver is a skilled committee chairman who understands how to arrange an agenda to ensure the despatch of business without too much argument. His critics dub this style high-handed and autocratic.

"He achieves a bland environment where in other places there might be a better, franker, discussion, 'but then technologists are a fairly docile lot in the main anyway', one lecturer says."

By the time of Chilver's retirement, Cranfield had developed from a college designed for about 100 students specialising in only aeronautics, via aeronautics and management courses in the late 1960s, into a degree-awarding, chartered institute of technology specialising mainly in post-graduate education in the sciences, engineering, technology and management.

An impressively high proportion of its income came from industry and commerce; in 1988 only 14 per cent of its £56.2million came from government grant. A further nine million pounds was earned by Cranfield's score of wholly-owned research companies which centred on 'the application of science' – to become a pivotal phrase in Cranfield's continuing development – and of technological expertise to research, design and development problems in industry and commerce.

Lord Chilver himself looks back on his Cranfield years with quiet satisfaction, emphasising that quality, in teaching and research, was a watchword of his time there: "At Bristol and Cambridge the lessons I learned were that the quality groups were the backbone of any institution. Unless you have quality, you probably cannot survive as an institution.

"I got the message again when I was a professor at University College, London. What I did there – and this was a turning-point for me – was to have a look at my own department of engineering to see whether we could get any external support for it, and by the time I left we had more money coming in from outside than we had from inside.

"Other heads of department were horrified," he told me. "But it was the first school at University College to achieve such a thing, and we were able to create Chairs. We raised enough money to fund a professor for life."

"I thought the idea had tremendous potential, and I'd made a study of Cranfield's potential before I accepted the job. I was, in fact, appointed Principal of the College of Aeronautics, because the job had not been determined when I came.

"Professor Murphy was made the first Vice-Chancellor, and it was very important that he should get that, because he had done an enormous amount, and I took over in 1970, and spent the first year or so bringing focus to Cranfield."

He explains: "One of the problems with many institutions is that you find the focus has been slowly diluted by time. So that was the important point, that we got down first to actually focusing, and instead of there being something like 10 or 20 different elements, who had all established their positions quite independently, we had a framework of definite areas."

Lord Chilver focused on the main fields of technological work: aeronautics, mechanical engineering, electrical engineering, materials, production and precision engineering. He built up the Management School as a group independent from the technologies - "and the acceptance of that principle was quite a turning-point" - and re-shaped the Faculty structure ("previously they had not made a real distinction between Faculties and Schools").

And he set targets: "At that time," he remembers, "universities were only just beginning to see that you had to set targets and couldn't just drift along. So I set targets, and you didn't really get cash until you reached them. It was a revolutionary step, a breath of fresh air."

Each department became self-financing, with its income depending on its success in generating commercial contracts and attracting students. The University's Government grant was shared out according to the number of students recruited and the honours classes of their first degrees. Each department then paid a "tax", according to the amount of office space, use of lecture theatres, electricity and to support other central services.

The Chilver philosophy was based on self-sufficiency. A head of department would tell him "Look, this is work of the very highest quality, work that is essential to this country". And Chilver would reply "You go and tell people out there about it then, and they'll beat a path to your door."

Slowly Cranfield achieved the position where the best departments were able to raise their own resources. "We didn't just have one wealth-generator," said Chilver, "but about 50. I told the heads 'I can't go and talk to every industry myself, but you can', and that was the revolutionary step. It had never been done before."

People underestimate the commercial prowess of the academic, Chilver believes. "An academic as a leader is very responsible, very numerate, and can actually understand accounts – which many people in industry cannot. It's quite intriguing. Some professors became extremely rich people."

On the taxation system he introduced, Lord Chilver says: "It was minimal, and the departments paid it willingly. They became very money-conscious and were able to retain their external finance. My view was that they had actually raised the money themselves – I hadn't – and they could keep it in their pockets.

"It was a pivotal thing for Cranfield, but it was anathema to Murphy. Some former colleagues would go to him and say 'That terrible man! Look what we've got to do now!' and he'd come to me and say 'It's going to ruin this place', and I'd say 'Well, if it ruins it, I'll get the sack. If, on the other hand, it succeeds, we'll be doing well'.

"But he couldn't accept that, and even Kings Norton got very worried at times. He'd say 'My goodness, that chap's got millions of pounds!' and I'd say 'That's what he's earned, and he's keeping it for a rainy day'. For the first time, they could actually store up investment for the future, which is what they did."

As *The Independent* put it: Lord Chilver is, according to Cranfield colleagues, good at backing new profit-making ventures but, if they fall on thin times, the umbrella of financial support is whisked away without ceremony. 'If you run out of research council money, you do not get propped up', says one academic. 'Certainly there are people who feel that they have had a raw deal because when they needed the umbrella they found that someone else had got it'.

Says Chilver: "I was either very popular or very unpopular, but the fact that the scheme grew enormously showed that was how they liked to do things."

Next, he turned his attention to funding building operations. This was more revolutionary thinking; at the time universities were dependent on the Government – on the Department of Education and Science – for finance for new buildings; sometimes there was money to be had, sometimes not. Chilver's view was that he had a very powerful, stable and successful institution, in existence since 1946: he saw it as a solid base on which to raise money.

Cranfield therefore became the first to borrow a large amount of money, in the region of half a million pounds. The first loan was for the building of student residences which, the Vice-Chancellor pointed out, would produce a steady income. According to Chilver, the finance committee was horrified, but in fact the loan was paid back before its time. It was the first in a stream of such schemes.

"It is interesting that the stock of buildings in British universities is in the order of £10-20billions," says Chilver, "and they don't know it. They have the most enormous borrowing power in the world, and yet they are only now beginning to follow the example we set."

After a few years, Lord Chilver set about promoting the objectives and services offered by the Schools to industry and commerce. That was the next turning-point, and yet another example of Cranfield's showing the way to other universities.

"I think it was one of the earliest exercises in the collective promotion of an institute," he says. First we needed publicity, and I went out to sell the idea, with lunches every day for key people from industry. I would put on the table a simple little document – not pretentious, nothing glossy – which was very pertinent to what we were doing and say 'Here's what we are doing – how can we help you?'

"I focused on business over lunch, and in the afternoon they would go into details with others at Cranfield. Slowly, the others became confident themselves, and started entertaining companies on their own."

This latest initiative coincided with Harold Wilson's 'white heat of technology' - "which wasn't in itself helpful to Cranfield, because Wilson actually overdid it. But interestingly the main proponent of Cranfield within the government was Tony Benn."

Benn – Anthony Wedgwood Benn – had sponsored the Charter for Cranfield. It had required the support of departments of government, and normally one of them would have been the Minister for Education, a position held at the time by Edward Short. Short, didn't sign it. "He was a terrible disappointment," recalls Chilver, "and that could have been the stumbling block. But Benn got hold of him and said 'Look, you are being absolutely bloody stupid here – this is what this country ought to be doing'.

"So we owe the future of Cranfield to Wedgie Benn. It was a terrible problem, but he did it, and so I was always a great supporter of Benn, and he was a good supporter of Cranfield."

The secret of the successful relationship had been in their first meeting, Chilver asked Benn how he saw the future of Cranfield, and how he thought it could relate to his plans. Benn's reply: "You are the first head of any British university who's asked if he can be of any help to me. Therefore we are going to take you up."

Relations with other areas of government were not to be so cordial, as Lord Chilver discovered when Cranfield set out to establish a special relationship, to culminate in double degrees, with the University of Compiègne, near Paris, in the late Seventies. "It was one of our most important international contacts," he says, "and unique in showing what two universities in different countries can do with each other.

"But the British, I found, were not helpful in strengthening that. It was done against every conceivable blockage by the British Government. British politicians were worried to death that they were going to give money to France, and they didn't want to know anything about it.

"I went to them and said 'Will you help me to make a formal relationship with Compiègne?' and they said 'No, because it's not in our power'. So I went to France myself and asked how we could formalise the arrangement.

"Eventually I went to their Minister of Research – they had a Minister of Research! - and asked him. He turned to his officials and asked 'What's against it?' and we got it through. But I was dreading him asking 'Can I meet the Minister on your side?' and so I got out quickly!"

Double-degree courses were offered in conjunction with Compiègne – the first of their type in Europe – and Lord Chilver was given an honorary degree by the French university. "The British Ambassador came along to the ceremony," he remembers, "and spoke, in beautiful French, of the massive support the British Government had given to the link."

Chilver was unable to resist taking the Ambassador to one side afterwards and suggesting that 'massive support' was perhaps just going over the top a little.' The Ambassador had to confess: "We're having terrible qualms about this. I know it was a complete disaster on our side, but what else could I say?"

And there, as Lord Chilver says, "you really see politics in action."

There were similar hiccups when Cranfield was discussing bringing Chinese students to Britain to take special courses designed to assist China's modernisation programme. "At this time I had a very able person called Alvan Davies working with me on this sort of thing," says Lord Chilver, "and he got wind that the Chinese were willing to locate some students in the West and to pay for it.

"He did a superb job in China, clearing the ground with the Chinese Embassy and so on, and I went with him to Peking to talk with the Chinese government. This was just after the Gang of Four business, and it was a very strained time.

"Everything had to be determined by the Vice-Premier, who was an old general, a marvellous chap, very amiable, and we were able to talk with him through interpreters. I hadn't noticed, but our talks had been filmed, and it was on television that evening. Our Ambassador there saw it and rang me at my hotel and asked 'What the hell's going on? Why didn't you tell me you were going to be here?'

"Actually I'd written to him six months before, saying I would conceivably be there and asking in what ways they could help us, and never had a reply to the letter. I told him

'You really ought to get your finger out!' and he took it very badly indeed."

The talks with the Chinese continued regardless. "It was a case of whether they trust you and you trust them," says Lord Chilver. "In China they say 'First of all, we'd like to become your friend' and they eye you up very carefully. They wanted special training for a group of young people who were already specialists – mainly in gas turbines and aeronautics – and eventually we enabled them to become experts in their fields.

"But of course we had problems over cash. I stuck out for the fees almost until our plane left, and I said to Alvan: 'We're not going to get this one, are we?' and he said 'You wait'. And as we got to the plane, a fellow came along with a piece of paper and we signed it.

"It meant that initially groups of 20 or 30 Chinese students came. We were the only country they did it with, and it was all very successful. But once again our government wanted to stay out of it, and in a way that teaches you to just get on and do it yourself. But on the other hand it's very undermining.

"The French bring their ambassador along and he goes all out for France, while our man finds reasons for not joining you, because he wants to stay neutral. It's very dispiriting, but you learn the technique of showing no sign of being dispirited. And when you come home you can only tell them that they're an absolute disaster."

From half way round the world, Chilver next turned his attention to the home scene. There was, he considered, no reason why Cranfield should remain a single campus institution. As it had diversified, so it could expand. Not all the staff were enthusiastic about this idea, but he says none was actually opposed to it.

Geographically, the one place that was obvious was the National College of Agricultural Engineering, founded in 1962 in Silsoe village, a short drive from Cranfield.

Chilver proposed to them a rationale, a scheme to strengthen their position, with relevant autonomy. Together, he argued, they could say they covered agriculture, food and high technology, and that probably in the next generation – although at the time he could only guess it – food science was going to be at least as equally important, if not more so, as some of the sciences being taught at Cranfield.

To those who wondered where might be the common links between agriculture and aerospace, it was explained that they were both centres of excellence, both at the forefront of their particular technologies, both concerned with the application of science, rather than merely the acquisition of the knowledge.

The success of the merger in 1974 was, said Chilver, based on relevant autonomy. "You optimise the autonomy between yourselves in order to get an effective and viable solution. That works every time." In 1988 Shuttleworth

College, an agricultural school established in memory of a wartime RAF pilot, Richard Shuttleworth, at Old Warden, Bedfordshire, also became a constituent of Cranfield.

There were new buildings at Cranfield for precision engineering ("very important, because that became a world leader") and then the beginnings of the relationship with the Royal Military College of Science at Shrivenham: "I had become chairman of the Advisory Committee at Shrivenham," Lord Chilver recalls, "and discovered they were thinking of getting together with another university.

"They asked me about Cranfield, and I thought it would be interesting to go for a massive contract to do this work, instead of for a grant, which is a pain when it doesn't work out – if they cut a grant, for example. So I suggested we have a contract with the Ministry of Defence to undertake academic and research work, and it was a great innovation.

"At first they said 'This won't appeal to anyone but Cranfield', and I said 'If you think so, open it up to competition'. They set up an independent group to review our case, and the result was that we won the first and biggest single contract anyone had placed in higher education in this country.

"It ran in the order of £10million a year, so in a period of 10 years that was £100million, and I believe the European potential of that is enormous."

There were several other landmarks in the Chilver years: "On the strength of our policies we got to the age of the new buildings at Cranfield. We rehoused Mechanical Engineering and improved computer services on all campuses. We developed the link with Shuttleworth, through Silsoe, and the CIM (Computer Integrated Manufacturing) Institute was extremely interesting, being funded entirely by industry. And more recently we saw policies which led to Cranfield becoming more autonomous."

Summing up that period, Lord Chilver says: "First we laid emphasis on the quality of teaching and research of direct interest to industry and commerce. And it's the quality that matters. I never have worried about numbers, and this puzzled lots of academics.

"They said 'Surely we have to produce more?', but I told them 'You just go for quality and the numbers will look after themselves'. And it worked. The numbers always went up. Quality was the generator.

"Secondly, we put emphasis on the relevant autonomy of the schools and research units to generate their own resources and deploy them. That was crucial, because what worried me very much about universities was not so much mismanagement as the lack of management, no management at all. They always see the head as an academic and the administrators as being second-class individuals who aren't qualified and not at the same level as academics, so they haven't got the concepts of development.

"Lastly, we achieved continuous growth of teaching and research throughout the period." All of which, Lord Chilver agrees, had not been easy or sometimes popular: "You must be ruthlessly commercial, I'm afraid," he says. "I always look to the returns in anything I do, and the best way to get a return is to invest in people."

———

EITHER VERY popular, or very unpopular, was how Chilver saw himself and certainly the Chilver years produced no little controversy. Archivist John Harrington says: "Commentators and critics of Chilver tend to divide fairly evenly into supporters and detractors.

"The former point to the undoubted growth of Cranfield, the enormous increase in its research and development income, and high reputation and esteem enjoyed by Cranfield's staff and students, the quality and relevance of its work and the extent of its activities and links overseas.

"Critics of Chilver accuse him of opportunism and a prevalence for planning for short-term advantage. He is credited, or blamed (depending on your point of view) with creating an atmosphere of competition, and an unshakeable belief in the relevance of market forces to education and research, which earned Cranfield the reputation as a model Thatcherite University during the 1980s."

And a very fine model indeed, according to one story: "It was before my time", recalls Professor Ron Fletcher, "but I'm told that Mrs Thatcher visited Cranfield when she was Minister for Education, and was met by a mob of students who'd come in from outside to demonstrate about something.

"But our guys, being older and more mature, simply picked them up and carried them off campus. Margaret Thatcher apparently had a very soft spot for Cranfield after that, and our next grant was supposed to be half a million more than we'd asked for!"

True? Lord Chilver comments: "Yes, I remember that occasion. It was a demo by outside students – and it certainly didn't do us any harm!"

Nor, according to many, did Chilver. Ron Fletcher again: "Henry Chilver's impact on the whole university scene has been colossal. He was very clever in simply saying 'All right, departments – you're on your own now'.

The key to the Chilver programme was giving autonomy to the schools and having taxation like a normal commercial venture, based on the head count of students. Schools and Colleges were taxed on space and all the other elements, just as in an ordinary business structure.

The system encouraged departments to generate more income, because they kept it themselves, and it encouraged them to make the best use of their resources. If they turned the lights out at night, they saved money for themselves. If they gave back space, they saved more money, and so on. And every penny they earned from outside consultancy and research, they kept.

The result was that those departments that could survive and grow independently did so, because they were not subsidising units that could not hack their own way; the uneconomic or impractical were closed or merged. Within five or six years the number of cost centres on Cranfield campus was reduced from fifteen to five, with the possibility of still further mergers.

Fletcher cites as an example the School of Automotive Studies: "It had been set up and was fully supported by the automotive industry, but as that industry went into decline in the UK, their support fragmented and it was considered no longer justified.

"The structure Henry Chilver set up is becoming quite common in universities. Everyone has sharpened up, and Cranfield was very much the model they followed. We led the way."

———

THE MAN who, in 1984, as Principal of the Royal Military College of Science, had helped Chilver bring Shrivenham into the University, was Professor Frank Hartley, a chemist who advised the Prime Minister on defence systems and the House of Lords on science and technology.

*Professor
Frank Hartley*

The son of a former Vice-Chancellor of the University of London, in 1989 he was offered the opportunity to succeed Chilver as Vice-Chancellor and was able to continue and to develop and to expand many of the innovations that had made Cranfield an excellent prototype for a modern university.

Under Hartley, indeed, Cranfield – one of the smallest higher education institutions in the UK – emerged as the biggest single earner of British industrial research funding. Within five years of his appointment Hartley was able to boast that Cranfield was earning fifty per cent more from industry than Imperial College, its nearest rival, and as much as Cambridge and Oxford combined.

Hartley gave Cranfield a mission statement: "to be a leading national, European and international institution for the advancement, dissemination and application of knowledge in Engineering, Applied Science, Manufacturing and Management in the industrial, commercial, rural, medical, defence and public sectors. Cranfield's particular mission is to transform world class science, technology and management expertise into viable practical, environmentally-desirable solutions that enhance economic development."

It is in fact a mission that Cranfield has managed to achieve.

"What we are all about," says Hartley, "is applying knowledge in the various sectors we have set out, and to have people coming to sponsor us in a big way, we need to be right up at the forefront of our subject and maintain ourselves there.

"It is that which has enabled us to develop the industrial activity we engage in, far beyond that of any UK university, despite the fact that we're very much smaller – and certainly much smaller in terms of government revenue size and numbers of academic staff – than any of the other universities that are significant competitors for industrial money."

In the mid-nineties, having consolidated Cranfield firmly at the leading edge in the industrial, commercial, public, rural and defence sectors, Hartley turned the University's attention, in a significant way, towards the medical and health sector.

"I don't see us ever developing a medical school, in the sense that a medical school is basically an undergraduate activity and needs linking with a major hospital," he says. "I think the UK has enough medical schools of that type, although if there is a case for more doctors, there could be a modest expansion of some or all of the existing schools.

"The area in which we can particularly contribute is in bringing engineering, applied science and management to the medical sector.

"If you look back ten or more years, and from ten to a hundred years back, there was a huge concentration of state-of-the-art medical schools in London. That made some sense, but not to the patients – because if you look at a normal hospital, almost whatever area you're in, 90 per cent of the patients have very routine things wrong with them.

"It's the other 10 per cent, and probably far less, who are actually interesting to medical science and of value in taking medicine forward. And if you're one of the interesting few and you live in Yorkshire, it's a bit hard if you have to go all the way to London to be treated.

"What we've seen recently is more being done in the regions, but inevitably that means that if you go into any hospital you've got relatively few patients needing state-of-the-art treatment.

"So what we've done so far is develop a link with Gloucester Royal Hospital, where they have some state-of-the-art medical groups, and we would hope to develop links with other hospitals in the future. We've created what we call a Centre of Post-graduate Medical Sciences in Gloucester, and we would hope to have a number of these centres in hospitals around the country, creating a School of Post-graduate Medical Sciences.

"But they cannot just be centred on Cranfield or Bedford or Milton Keynes or Shrivenham or Swindon. We have to get a much bigger catchment area than that if we are to have top surgeons and top clinicians working with our scientists."

Health was not a new interest for Cranfield, where medical electronics had been researched, and the findings successfully applied to practical advantage, for some time. One application, in biotechnology, had been to introduce body fluids to an electrode, producing a signal which is a number.

As Professor Hartley put it, "We started with glucose levels for diabetics – you prick your thumb, get some blood, stick it on to something that looks not unlike a ball-point pen and up comes your number, like the date comes up on some fancy pens, giving your glucose level.

"Well, that sounds brilliant, but the problem is having to put a hole in your thumb, putting blood on a gauge and reading it. So the ultimate stage to take a device like that is to insert an electrode somewhere in the body and get a continuous reading, which might come out on something like a wristwatch, so the glucose level can be checked all the time. If you're a diabetic and you don't react quickly enough, you pass out. So the ideal would be a permanent system that is going all the time.

"It would be of great benefit to many people, because there are diabetics of varying ability and intelligence, and most would have no difficulty in responding to the warning sign coming up on the wristwatch."

Another application of science being examined at Gloucester is the use of lasers in the treatment of cancers.

"In some cases to actually cut out the cancerous section can have a high-mortality rate, whereas with a laser you can either stop the cancer growing or even burn it out, without causing anything like the trauma to the whole body."

That was the biggest new area Cranfield was likely to enter said the Vice-Chancellor. "But we're also seeing some of our older areas merging. For example, we used to work in the private sector and the public sector quite distinctly. Now the public sector is learning huge amounts from the private sector, and indeed the private sector is learning somewhat from the public sector. So the old boundaries are merging.

"I suppose 20 years ago there was very little that agriculture and defence had in common, but it's surprising how much, potentially, they do have in common, and one of the areas we're working on at Silsoe is called precision farming.

"With this, you find out what you need to put in the field – herbicides, insecticides or whatever – to either control weeds or insects, but you put the right amount in the right place in the field and don't just spray haphazardly. That's economically very good news for the farmer, and environmentally very good news for people like the National Rivers Authority.

"It's exactly the same satellite positioning technology as was used in the Gulf War and to some extent in the Falklands and in Bosnia. So defence and farming, which used to be poles apart, are now very strongly linked.

"And it's quite interesting that the very first conference I opened after I brought Shrivenham into Cranfield was a joint one between Shrivenham and Silsoe on land soils," he says.

"They'd discovered that farmers wanted to go across soils with the minimum of damage and weren't so concerned about speed, while the military were desperately keen to cross land quickly, and weren't too particular about the damage that could mean. So they tried to characterise how you do minimum damage on the one hand, and how you get maximum speed on the other, and by putting the problems together could come up with an answer for both requirements.

"So new sectors, but merging sectors, I see as a significant part of our way forward, helping us generate income. The amount we get from the Government through Funding Council is modest, so we see ourselves as having to earn in the market place the bulk of our income, some 82 per cent.

"We serve the industrial, commercial, defence and public sectors at Cranfield, the rural sector at Silsoe and Shuttleworth, the defence, public and medical sectors at Shrivenham and the medical sector at Gloucester. We serve them in two ways – teaching or education of students on degree and mid-career development courses, and through our research.

"And we see that going on in to the indefinite future, because if you become too dependent on any one source of funding, whether it be government or any individual sponsor, you end up with too few decision-makers out there and you're very susceptible to somebody having a bright idea of doing whatever he's been doing with you in a different way tomorrow."

Too few clients, too little diversification, means that the University is hostage to the whims of individuals, however well-intentioned. The 1957 White Paper, however ostensibly disastrous for the original vision of Cranfield solely as a College of Aeronautics, was therefore a blessing in disguise: it gave Cranfield no alternative but to diversify.

"Aeronautics and aerospace technology are not cheap subjects either to teach or to research; nor are aircraft and dedicated airfields cheap to run. It is unlikely that Cranfield would have survived on such a restricted regime as "aerospace", especially in a country that for years has had no realistic space programme. When I arrived the College of Aeronautics was running at a loss, and pulling the rest of the University down with it, but it had provided a solid base on which to build – and from which to diversify.

"That diversification has given us a more robust way ahead," says Hartley. "And it also means that as a university we are more closely linked to the economy – not just the UK economy, but the world economy – than a typical UK university. We live in the commercial and business world much more than they do."

He said: "When I took over, I pondered long and hard as to whether or not we should create a school specifically concerned with environmental issues. I concluded we should not, because every part of the University has a major contribution to make to improving the environment and ensuring that its students when they leave undertake their future activities in such a way that they enhance and certainly do not damage the environment."

A little-known example of Cranfield's concern for the environment is the aircraft that actually monitors upper atmosphere pollution from industry and power stations over the UK and parts of Europe. It is owned and operated by the University, and its equipment was supplied and installed by Cranfield.

Jet aircraft cause damage to the upper atmosphere, particularly the ozone layer, through the products of combustion they leave behind. The world's leading clean combustion centre for gas turbines is at Cranfield, funded by Rolls-Royce, the National Economic Development Office of Japan, Johnson Matthey and the EC.

Cranfield staff at Cranfield and Silsoe research almost every aspect of water resources, their management and quality. At farm and water catchment levels the focus is on the integrated protection and management of soil and water. Aspects of the UK's national groundwater protection have been developed by the University, which is among the world's leaders in land-based techniques for protecting surface waters from agrochemicals, organic wastes, landfills and sediment.

World-wide, Cranfield staff are involved in rural clean water supply for local communities and agriculture, the rehabilitation of wells for drinking water, and the control of polluting run-off from land.

Many of the University's separate schools, centres and departments are concerned with differing aspects of transport which is of significant environmental concern and Cranfield's multi-disciplinary transportation research is designed to contribute to a better understanding of the interaction between transport and current environmental problems.

The Vice-Chancellor says: "Strategic transport development, quality of life, 'green' taxes, and the movement of freight and people by land, sea and air are all subjects on which we undertake research and teaching. I'd say we have environmental issues pretty well covered."

AS CRANFIELD developed the old RAF site into an ultra modern technical university the Mid-Bedfordshire District Council and the Bedfordshire County Council came to recognise its importance as a nucleus for local economic development and began both actively and financially supporting an initiative for an Innovation Centre on the Technology Park.

The Technology Park itself had developed from a vague idea into a practicality when Nissan, the Japanese car manufacturing giant, foresaw the opportunity of basing itself beside Cranfield during 1989.

Nissan executives had considered more than 200 possible sites across Europe and narrowed it down to just three or four. They had even motored around the campus at night, to get a feel for the place. In the end, they opted for a university association, and decided to site the company's third Technology Centre – others in Tokyo and Detroit cover the Far East and American markets – on the edge of the Cranfield campus .

The first phase, covering 9,700 square metres on a 20-acre site, was completed in Autumn, 1991, and the second of 10,000 square metres in the Spring of 1993, and now all Nissan's European cars are designed at Cranfield for manufacture in Washington and Spain. The company employs about 350 people on site and is investing some £45million at Cranfield. Not surprisingly, Nissan is regarded as the "front door" of the Technology Park.

The Park is emerging as a dedicated research, design and development site with advanced training facilities, all fully compatible with the University's own mission. Its aim is to attract national and international industries and public sector organisations involved in high technology research, design, development and training.

"It is there to do two things," says Professor Fletcher. "To generate income and attract to campus those people we want to do business with. It would be very exciting if we could bring here some more big players like Nissan. But we are now negotiating our next step forward with an Innovation Centre, to attract young high-technology companies, too."

The Innovation Centre is planned to provide space for small to medium-sized knowledge-based companies, as well as the kind of support small companies need – flexible property to allow them to grow, and services and advice to help them run their businesses. Some of the companies will undoubtedly be spin-outs from the University, but others will wish like Nissan to relocate to Cranfield to gain the benefits of links with the University.

The experience with Innovation Centres at other Universities has been that they are catalysts in the successful development of Science and Technology Parks, thereby promoting the creation of long-term sustainable jobs in the area and the likelihood is that the most successful companies will expand out of the Innovation Centre on to the main Technology Park, so that the process becomes self-generating in terms of building up the opportunities on the Park and in the surrounding area.

The Vice-Chancellor said: "In the past the Government has funded the development of universities. That, however, is historic. Regardless of which Party wins the next few General Elections, it is extremely unlikely that any government will be prepared to pay to either develop, replace or even maintain university buildings and facilities.

"It will be up to the universities to fund this themselves, through their own assets. Thus while we believe that developments such as the Technology Park are good for our academic work through the interactions that occur, and good for job creation in the community, they are also vital if we are to keep our over 50-year-old campus maintained properly, let alone developed.

"In 1990 we had to spend £1million on our runway, two years ago a third of a million on our sewage works, this year £1million on our HV electricity ring main. So just maintaining the University is expensive; developing it further is even more so."

———

HIGH PRAISE has been heaped on Cranfield's new library and the architect responsible for it, Sir Norman Foster, and the story behind its building deserves a place in any Cranfield history.

Originally there were two libraries on campus – one covering Management, housed in an area on the first floor of the Business School, and the other covering Science and Technology on the first floor of the Stafford Cripps building.

Cranfield's

multi award-winning

library

They were far from ideal, and the Stafford Cripps library was "particularly depressing", Librarian John Blagden wrote in a feature for *New Library World*. "There was no lift, poor lighting and a motley collection of furniture and shelving. Both libraries were chronically short of reader seating."

What's more, more than half of the library's material had to be kept in stores in various locations, bringing delays and

difficulties for those who needed it. The problem could only grow, and so a new library became a priority in the capital building programme.

A case for it was made to the Department of Education and Science, who in 1984 provided funds for a feasibility study to evaluate potential sites and the nature and size of a new library building. But it was not until five years later that the funds became available – a total of £7.5million, with some £4million to cover the cost of the building.

Six firms were short-listed for the work, all architects were interviewed, and the Library Building Committee unanimously chose Sir Norman Foster and Partners. There were 10 people involved in the selection process, and John Blagden says: "I suspect each member of the committee had a slightly different set of reasons for selecting Fosters".

Two reasons which led most to choose Fosters, he believes, were the quality of their buildings – especially the Sainsbury Centre at the University of East Anglia and the model of the Mediatheque at Nîmes – and the effectiveness of their presentation.

But "one other factor which certainly influenced some members of the selection committee was that the Fosters team arrived by helicopter, piloted by Sir Norman. It became very clear that Sir Norman was fascinated by aeroplanes and had a genuine interest in aerospace technology. It was this interest that reinforced the empathy between client and architect which was so important to the success of the project."

In the Spring of 1990, a presentation made to staff and students of the proposed design was generally well received, and in 1994 Blagden could report on reactions after the first year of occupancy: "It is interesting to note that more controversy was generated by the sculptures and paintings which the Hayward Gallery agreed to lend Cranfield than any issue connected with the building.

"Katherine Gili's Vertical 111 was singled out for some particularly virulent comments, but even here, according to a students' union survey, 25 per cent of students were favourably impressed by the selection".

In fact, he added, "the majority of users have commented very favourably on the new library. What most users seem to like particularly is the openness of the facilities, the high degree of visibility and accessibility of staff and the restful, tranquil nature of the colour schemes.

"Users comment favourably on the use of natural light, in contrast to so many traditional libraries, with their heavy brick or masonry structures in which readers sit in horseboxes, under banks of oppressive artificial light.

"Some find the Foster aesthetic antiseptic and cold, others liken the building to a Ben Nicolson painting, an exercise in cool, restrained lyricism." But the national and professional Press were almost unanimous in their praise.

"Cranfield's library", declared *The Guardian*, "is the perfect example of a mature Foster building. Every piece is beautifully made, every proportion is effortlessly right, every tone is an essay in tasteful grey restraint."

More praise came from *Building* magazine: "Cranfield now has at its heart a building that expresses the advanced technologies of the Institute in which aeronautics is still a prime subject. The new library building revels in the use of modern technological materials such as glass, steel, aluminium and concrete."

There was a prediction in *The Independent on Sunday* that "the building of the year might well be Sir Norman Foster and Partners' new library for Cranfield", and they were not wrong: in October 1993 the Construction Industry Association and the *Daily Telegraph* presented Cranfield with the Building of the Year award, and the accolade of the supreme construction project of the year.

Said Blagden: "The library building is quite dramatic and in sharp contrast to many other buildings on the campus. Staff and students, therefore, feel compelled to take a view on the building, not as a library but as an exercise in monumentality.

"There are those who will always be antipathetic to modern architecture and those who will support modernity come what may. I believe, however, that the project team has persuaded a significant number of Cranfield staff and students that modern buildings can be both functionally effective and beautiful."

The Visionary Application of Science

Visitors to Cranfield in the summer of 1995 may easily have left the campus blissfully unaware of the developments that had taken place in the field of pilot vision in the fifty years since pilots were pedalling around the parade ground.

New technology enables a computer to "see" through a pilot's eyes, and to identify which instruments he is watching – or not watching.

It started with the discovery that the brain is aware of the rate of flicker observed by the eye but unrecorded in human consciousness, when, for example, working under a neon light; next, that a sensor placed underneath the scalp, on the flat part at the back of the skull, could monitor that rate. What Cranfield thinks of as the visionary application of knowledge, and advertisers as the appliance of science, was to put a use to that discovery.

The avionics department within the College of Aeronautics experimented by introducing varying rates of flicker to different instruments in a simulated cockpit display and attaching a computer to the sensor beneath the scalp. This system showed on screen precisely which of his controls the pilot was watching, and for how long – and which he was ignoring, and for how long. Later, it was discovered that a felt tip, as used in some modern pens, when fitted inside a flying helmet and positioned to rest on the appropriate part of the skull, could monitor the rate of flicker without the need to penetrate the scalp, and regardless of the amount of hair on a pilot's head.

The technology, being pursued in conjunction with British Aerospace, has obvious "black box" implications; more importantly, by making a pilot aware that he may be neglecting vital controls, it could prevent fatal accidents.

The idea of being able to see patterns of darkness and light as they are observed by a pilot brings science fiction ever closer to reality: photography is, after all, only a measurement of differing degrees of light.

At Silsoe, existing defence technology – exactly the type that directed missiles and pilots during the Gulf War and in Bosnia – has been developed to guide tractors and combine harvesters across fields of cereals.

Satellite positioning, which many yachtsmen rely on as GPS, or know generically as "Decca", is fitted to combines as they traverse fields and by measuring the amount of crop harvested in each position will produce a contour-like map showing the varying yields for precise areas of farmland.

The School of Agriculture, Food and Environment has developed the knowledge as precision farming; for the farmer feeds the map back into the GPS when he drives out, this time on his tractor, and delivers an appropriate amount of fertiliser to maximise the production capability of his acreage.

Perhaps uniquely, precision farming brings together all the elements in which Cranfield specialises: aerospace and defence technology, engineering, materials, management, chemical development, and the environment.

What today's visitor may readily notice on Cranfield campus is a now sadly-neglected Trident aircraft, not far from the former hangar in which students receive their degrees. It was in that aeroplane that researchers from the Applied Psychology Unit established what went wrong in the Manchester air disaster: why what should have been an injury-free survivable accident killed so many people. In fact virtually every aspect of aviation safety from design stage to the cockpit layout through to the passenger cabin and into the airport has been enhanced by the work of the APU.

Some years ago Cranfield converted a Hawk aircraft to fly-by-wire. This pioneering technology lies at the heart of today's Airbus aircraft. The pilot tells a computer which direction he wishes to go – in simple terms, up, down, left or right. The computer then takes over and trims the aircraft and adjusts the power.

In 1995, visitors to No. 2 Hanger could have seen that technology being installed into the formidable Harrier and, in a similar aircraft beside it, the next generation of this technology being developed by Cranfield University engineers – fly-by-light, replacing the copper wires of fly-by-wire with fibre optic cables.

Pursuing the Chancellor's historic responsibility for providing the engineering and administrative support to Sir Frank Whittle as he developed the jet engine, the University claims that no Rolls-Royce jet engine has ever been developed in which Cranfield engineers and students have not been responsible for at least one key component. In the late nineties much of the work is focused on environmentally clean combustion to power the Concorde successor, work that is heavily funded by the Japanese Government as well as Rolls-Royce and which contributes significantly to the balance of payments through export earnings.

The School of Management is now one of the top in Europe for the development of middle and senior management. In a survey conducted by an American magazine in the mid-nineties the School was voted second-best in the world for its work in companies. Companies from all over the world send their top executives to Cranfield to develop their future strategies and provide the education and training needed to implement them.

When the Higher Education Funding Council for England carried out, in 1994, its first assessment of university teaching, it opted to examine Cranfield's mechanical engineering and management and concluded that the teaching of both disciplines was excellent.

A modern space telescope such as that on Hubble has a mirror fifty metres, about two cricket pitches, in diameter. It has to be made in segments, packed and then rebuilt in space. Only one place in the world, Cranfield, has the technology to grind the components of such a mirror so accurately that they can be assembled into a single mirror in space.

Cranfield scientists developed the underwater welding techniques so essential to exploration in the North Sea, and they are now developing new welding systems to enable welding to be undertaken at phenomenal depths – 2500 metres – under water so paving the way for the opening of new oilfields.

Cranfield expertise is as vital to land as it is to outer space and ocean depths. Many farmers make vital use of soil maps of their farms, courtesy of surveys conducted by the Soil Survey and Land Research Centre at Silsoe. The University's soil and water engineers are involved world-wide with almost every major environmental and agricultural programme from Brogburgh in Bedfordshire to the centre for Arid Zone Studies that Cranfield runs in Maiduguri on the edge of the Sahara in Northern Nigeria.

At Shrivenham Cranfield trains United Nations inspectors to detect biological and chemical warfare factories. And when disaster strikes anywhere in the world, whether an air crash, famine, flood or drought, the likelihood is that those responding will have been taught their skills by Cranfield, or trained by those who learned them there. One nation that did not seek the University's advice was Japan. But after the disastrous earthquake at Kobe and following the terrorist nerve gas attack on the Tokyo underground, Vice-Chancellor Frank Hartley found himself invited to spend time with Japan's National Police Authority in Tokyo.

Cranfield prides itself on fifty years spent making things happen, and sometimes in helping make sure that things need never happen again.

——

A CHANCE remark by the Princess Royal launched a Cranfield charity that has brought relief, help and hope to many thousands of people world-wide – the Cranfield Trust.

At Cranfield's 40th anniversary celebrations, Princess Anne mentioned that, as Patron of the Save the Children Fund, she had come to realise how many charities needed help with technology as well as with their management and organisational skills.

Some members of Convocation, Cranfield's alumni association, thought over her remark, and soon afterwards the Cranfield Trust was established as a registered charity, with the Princess as its patron, to help other charities in Britain and around the world in need of technical expertise.

Its objectives were to provide pre-disaster planning – by, for example, investigating hypothetical or past disasters that may recur – providing logistical, technical and agricultural solutions to problems, and to suggest or develop solutions to problems associated with relief in Third World and developed countries.

The Trust has access to a vast reservoir of talent drawn from Cranfield's excellence in aeronautics, agriculture, electrical and mechanical engineering, transport and logistics and management, and draws on volunteers – currently more than 300 – from graduates, staff and students.

Much of its early work was in helping charities overseas, but the Cranfield Trust can, and does, tackle almost anything and everything.

"We provide sharply-focused help, free of charge," they say, "to other charities to assist them with specific problems of a management, logistical or technical nature. In this way, we firstly enable their budgets to go further, as they do not need to buy in alternative help – even assuming they could find it: some problems are very eclectic.

"Second, as a result of our inputs, we allow their scarce resources to be more efficiently put to use at the sharp end – whether this be servicing disabled people from London, caring for the old and sick in Yugoslavia, motivating deprived youngsters in Scotland or feeding refugees from Rwanda. All we ask is that our client charities be involved in the relief of human deprivation and suffering."

Once, officials recall, community nurses working in remote villages in the Gambia were given motorcycles to help them get around. It was a generous gesture, but the bikes had quickly become useless on the rough terrain, and there were problems maintaining the machines and in getting spare parts. So a Trust volunteer went out to teach the nurses exactly how to ride and maintain their bikes in the conditions they faced.

At home, the Trust has helped small and relatively new charities with personnel, accounting and computer systems, and one of its flagship projects was a portable vaccine refrigerator which a group of students from the School of Mechanical Engineering helped design.

Giving a personal perspective of just one year's work (for 1993-94) Trust Chief Executive Maggie Heraty reported: "Early in 1994 we were asked by the World Health Organisation for advice on the provision of gas supplies to hospitals, orphanages and old people's homes in Serbia.

"Our specialist volunteer reported that lack of heating, hot water and sterilisation facilities were contributing to loss of life among the most vulnerable of the civilian population. As a result of his input, which identified how to segregate gas supplies for humanitarian purposes, sanctions were waived by the UN."

In March 1994, she added, "we returned to the site of two of our earliest projects, Ethiopia, when we supplied the Team Leader for a mission by Save the Children. He and his team assessed the roads and transport system in northern Ethiopia and recommended improvements to cater for SCF's food and medical distribution system in a predicted further famine.

"Then the Rwandan emergency struck, and throughout the summer we were very intensively involved, mostly through the Logistics and Transport Section of the UN High Commissioner for Refugees. The scale of the disaster was overwhelming; it seemed that every day there was a new call for help, advice and information from agencies wanting help or seeking to give it.

"In terms of mobilising volunteers, we supplied five specialists to run transport and logistics for different parts of UN-HCR's relief operation in Zaire and Rwanda itself, and one to manage the UN staff accommodation in Goma, Zaire."

But despite all that, most of the Trust's work was done in the UK: some 100 projects were started, completed or still ongoing during the year, during which 30 volunteers were active at any one time.

Looking Back to the Future

CRANFIELD DEGREES are highly sought after in the worlds of industry, commerce and academia; but Cranfield graduates receive more than a certificate of achievement when they are presented with their degrees: they get to touch history. Every degree awarded to Cranfield graduates has been presented, with a congratulatory handshake, by the Chancellor, Lord Kings Norton, whose range of achievements is sweeping and astonishing, from designing the R101 airship (and, furiously, being denied a place on its ill-fated proving flight) to introducing America to the jet age and acting as "entrepreneur" for his friend Frank Whittle.

He met and spoke with Orville Wright. He helped devise the kite barrage balloons which brought down Germany's wartime V1 missiles, and has helped make flying safer and faster for everyone: "Anyone who flies," says one biographical sketch writer, "is to some extent in his debt."

Not least, though, Lord Kings Norton of Wotton Underwood was, among a small group of determined visionaries, a prime mover for and founder of Cranfield, to which he has been father figure, guiding light, first and only Chancellor from 1969 and champion since the start.

"I have been in the service of Cranfield for 50 years," he said on Graduation Day in 1995. "Beyond that, my only aim is the Guinness Book of Records." And if not there, it is fitting that the last words in this history should be his, for his were among the first, half a century ago.

Yet suggest that his is the story of aviation, that he has been there at every stage of its incredible development and has known all its major players, from Orville Wright to Whittle and beyond, and he merely shrugs and smiles: "Well, I can cover the ground."

There is some ground to cover, beginning with the birth of Harold Roxbee Cox in Birmingham on June 6, 1902, a few months after Wilbur Wright addressed engineers in Chicago on the possibility of powered flight, before he and his brother began examining wing profiles, using a bicycle as a test platform.

As a boy, like many at that time, Roxbee Cox was bitten by the flying bug, and vividly remembers being taken by his father to air shows, pageants and races at places like Edgbaston and Bournville, where magnificent men showed off their flying machines, thrilling vast crowds with feats of skill and daring.

"So I was interested in aviation from my very early days," he says, and it is hardly surprising that he was working in the industry soon after leaving Kings Norton Grammar School: "I had an extraordinarily successful time as a schoolboy, and my headmaster wanted me to do chemistry and go to Birmingham University.

"Well, I didn't want to do chemistry, so I persuaded my father to let me leave school, and at 16 I was able to join the aircraft design department of the Austin motor company at Longbridge. They had already designed one or two successful aeroplanes, and I was happily engaged with the flight trials of a new bomber they'd just finished and in the design of the very first light aeroplane.

"We designed the Austin Whippet, which flew in 1919. It had a steel cube fuselage, folding wings and all sorts of novelties. It really was, for those days, a tremendous step forward, and we built six of them.

"Then of course, came the great recession of 1921, and although by that time we had flown another sporting two-seater, a lovely aeroplane called the Kestrel, it was really all over for aeroplanes at Austin's."

From the drawing office, the young designer went to work with apprentices in the works and maintenance shops and toolroom, all the time studying for an external London University BSc which he achieved with first-class honours.

In 1922 he left Austin for Imperial College - "a really wonderful institution" - to do research work for his PhD, before facing one of the most exciting and challenging tasks of his career, working with the small team designing the government-financed R101 airship at Cardington in Bedfordshire.

"I was the first recruit to the team in 1924," he remembers, "and when I was being taken around what was called the lofting room, I saw men bending long thin pieces of wood and keeping them in position with weights.

"Naturally I asked 'What are those men doing?' and was told 'They're producing the shape of the ship; that's the way we design ships'. I said: 'All you need is an equation so you can calculate all that', and I produced one.

"In fact four of us did it all, devised the whole system of calculation, and it was absolutely comprehensive. And what a mess we should make of it all today, with all those computers, when four of us, working with cylindrical slide-rules, did the whole darned thing!

"We had some junior chaps working on more basic calculations under our guidance, but we couldn't do better today than we did then. We should just use more people, a lot of computers and a lot of information which was no good at all.

"It probably sounds like a silly old Conservative talking, but it isn't quite like that. I think the silicone chip is absolutely amazing, and I depend quite a lot on it, as we all do, but in that particular case we should not have done any better and might have done a lot worse.

"Basically, you can't get more out than you put in. So" - he laughs - "I don't think we need worry about being controlled by robots. We'd lick them any day!"

Despite producing the outline shape – a mathematical closed curve – of the R101, Roxbee Cox was denied his fervent wish to travel on the proving flight from Cardington to Egypt and India in October, 1930.

"When it was nearly finished," he recalls, "the man in charge of production, A. E. Hall, was sent to be superintendent at the Royal Aircraft Establishment in Farnborough, and he said he must have me with him. And although the ship had not flown, I was a civil servant and was moved, willy-nilly, to Farnborough.

"I was still quite desperate to go on the flight and wrote to the Director of Airship Development about it, but he said there were too many 'me, too's', very important people, going, and I could go on the second flight. I've still got that letter.

"Well of course there wasn't a flight after it, so here I am! But I was desperately disappointed not to go, and I will never forget the day it flew. My wife and I were living in an hotel at Farnborough and had no radio, but we picked up a newspaper and there was the appalling news."

In what was then the worst disaster in British aviation history, the 777ft R101 crashed a few hours out from Cardington, killing 48 passengers and crew, including the

Secretary of State for Air, Lord Thomson, as it hit the ground in Beauvais, northern France, and turned into a fireball. Only six passengers escaped.

The airship had first hit trouble over the Channel when it was forced low by a faulty engine and rain. Over France, still flying very low, it pitched and rolled, then dived, levelled out and plunged to earth.

"So many people were tragically killed," says Lord Kings Norton, "that I was one of the few left who could get the airship programme going again." He became Chief Technical Officer at the Royal Airship Works, and there were plans to continue with the R100, which had flown the Atlantic and back.

"Then came one of those economy committees, which squashed the whole thing flat, and the R100 was scrapped. I think it was a combination of economy and the R101 disaster. Without that, there would have been an airship programme, although it would have eventually disappeared, because the aircraft was overtaking it.

"But the Germans did not give up as easily as we did, and did not lose a passenger until the Hindenburg in 1937. I did not fly in that, but I had a memorable flight in the Graf Zeppelin, from what is now Heathrow to Friedrichshafen. It was a most thrilling experience."

Although Lord Kings Norton dismisses occasional forecasts that airships might some day make a big comeback ("They have a very limited future indeed, I think"), he is still fascinated by them and by balloons, which rise from his coat of arms and from prints and pictures and maps, mugs, plates and coasters at his beautiful old home in the Cotswolds. His collection of prints on the subject is among the finest in the country. "Balloons are great fun things," he says. "I've much enjoyed flying in them, and hope to do so again."

Dr Roxbee Cox was still very much a committed airship man when he went, "somewhat reluctantly," back to Farnborough to work on the development of aeroplanes – and made an important contribution to air safety by studying the problems of flutter, which had caused accidents with fighters and light commercial aircraft.

His vital work on the problem, which in extreme cases could cause an aileron, wing or tailplane to fail in mid-air, was embodied in all future aircraft. So, too, were his studies on the stability and stiffness of wing structures, carried out with his former R101 colleague Alfred (later Sir Alfred) Pugsley, with whom he coined the phrase aeroelasticity.

After a term as Principal Scientific Officer in the Aerodynamics Department in Farnborough between 1935-6, Roxbee Cox became head of the Air Defence Department, and with his team devised the kite balloon barrage which thwarted many V1 missiles over southern England during the Second World War.

In 1938, as Chief Technical Officer to the Air Registration Board, his extensive structural experience was focused on the airworthiness of light aircraft, heralding requirements which became the standards manufacturers must meet.

The following year he was back again at Farnborough as Superintendent of Scientific Research, and in 1940 came the most important challenge of his career, vital to Britain's aero engine industry.

It brought him into close contact with Frank Whittle, "a truly great man," who since 1935 had been pressing the case for the jet engine – the aircraft gas turbine – often in the face of official indifference.

"I first knew him almost at the beginning of the War," says Lord Kings Norton, "and became very interested in the development of the Whittle engine.

"I was Deputy Director of Scientific Research at the Air Ministry, which was being changed into the Ministry of Aircraft Production, and became Director of Special Projects, which was a title to hide the fact that I was in charge of the Whittle engine, bringing in other firms to help."

Roxbee Cox realised that to gain the maximum advantage for Britain, all the country's engine manufacturers, including Whittle's Power Jets company, must exchange information about their various jet engine projects initiated during the War.

"Curiously, Whittle had his detractors," he says, "because there was always a bunch of conservatives – with a lower-case c – who didn't believe it could possibly work. Even A. A. Griffith, another great man, really did not believe it could work, although in the end he designed a gas turbine engine himself.

"So Whittle had to fight to get his ideas accepted, and fortunately there were some who did accept them, but not many in important positions. It's alleged that, at that time, I said 'Well, I'm on the side of the angels, but there aren't many angels in high places'. And that was true.

"In the end, though, I had some great allies, and I invented the Gas Turbine Collaboration Committee, to which all the people had to come if we were to make a production job of gas turbines. They were persuaded to put their ideas on the table, after I told them they could patent them before disclosing them.

"And we had a very successful committee, with firms like Rolls-Royce, Metropolitan-Vickers, Haldford-de Havilland, Armstrong-Siddeley, Bristol, Lucas and Ricardo all contributing. But there was this awful business in which it was felt in high places that Whittle could not be head of a great production firm.

"Well, I never knew why he couldn't be, but in the end the job was in effect handed over to Rover, who had some very good people. They wanted to make changes to the engine, and there was this terrific enmity built up between Whittle and his team and the Rover team under Maurice Wilkes, and in the end I did a deal with Spencer, Maurice's elder brother.

"The effect was that Rover took over the tank-engines and Rolls-Royce were the primary developers of the Whittle engine. They offered Whittle a good job, but it wasn't good enough for Frank, and he was probably right. They'd have looked after him, but he'd never have been quite happy.

"And although he's now heaped with honours beyond any possible further honour – he has an OM, the Order of Merit – and of course we gave him an honorary degree, which he treasures because he liked Cranfield and had friends there – he is only an Air Commodore in the RAF. God knows why they didn't make him an honorary Air Marshal, but they never have. It's a very curious thing."

Dr Roxbee Cox could, though, add his personal and public tribute to Frank Whittle (with whom he continued to keep in touch at his home in America): "I wrote a letter about him which I think I'm prouder of than anything I have ever done," he says.

"It was after the War, when the Royal Commission on Awards to Inventors was sitting, with two outstanding cases before them – Watson-Watt for radar and Whittle with the jet engine. I was asked to make an appraisal for the committee of Whittle's achievements, and I wrote a letter which I think has been quoted in nearly every book about him."

It read, in part: "Whittle's contribution was the association of jet propulsion and the gas turbine. Before him the gas turbine had been regarded, like other turbines, as a machine for supplying shaft power. Whittle recognised it as an ideal means of providing jet propulsion for aircraft... It is one thing to have an idea. It is another to have the technical and executive ability to give it flesh. It is still another to have the tenacity of purpose to drive through to success unshaken in confidence, in the face of discouraging opposition.

"Whittle, whose name in the annals of engineering comes after those of Watt, Stephenson and Parsons only for reasons of chronology or alphabetical order, had these things.

"It may be said that without Whittle the jet propulsion engine and the other applications of the turbine would have come just the same. They would. But they would have come much later. Whittle's work gave this country a technical lead of two years...

"So far the gas turbine has been generally regarded as a means of propulsion of fighting aircraft. I think posterity will see it rather as a great commercial asset, presuming that we today do our duty in exploiting it. They will see too that the initiative in its development came from aeronautical technologists, and at the head of them they will see Whittle."

It was a prophetic endorsement of Whittle's work, and the committee decided he should receive £100,000, the highest award to an inventor of the War years.

America also had great reason to thank Whittle, and Roxbee Cox: in July 1941, five months before the United States entered the War, they were first told the secrets of the jet engine. "And the awful thing is that I am the man who told them," confesses Lord Kings Norton with a mischievous grin. "I'm the betrayer. That's why I've got a high American decoration."

He explains: "Whittle published his first patent in January 1930 and put it to the Air Ministry, but got no support for building anything. They didn't bother to keep it secret, and the Germans started working on it. So although the jet engine was very much a British invention, the people who first exploited it were the Germans, and the Americans knew nothing about it. They just weren't on to it."

All that changed at a London meeting on July 22 1941 when Dr Roxbee Cox and Air Marshal F. J. Linnell briefed two American officials on the work of Power Jets, and later took them to meet Whittle and his workers. Soon afterwards, at the Gloster factory, they were shown the two prototype E28/39 aircraft in which the Whittle engine first flew, and a Whittle engine and its inventor went to America to assist its entry into the jet age.

"They picked it up pretty quickly," Lord Kings Norton recalls. "The Bell company built an aeroplane with two Whittle engines within a year, from start to finish. That was an amazing job."

His own role in that close co-operation was highlighted after the War, when Dr Roxbee Cox gave the ninth Wright

Brothers Lecture (and, incidentally, met Orville: "He had become rather eccentric by then, and was far more interested in his theories on money than he was in aircraft").

Colonel Donald Keirn, a US liaison officer on the engine programme, said at that time: "The great progress made in the few years of war, and the present excellence of several British gas turbines, could not have been achieved but for the whole-hearted way in which various firms interchanged know-how through the medium of the collaboration committee.

"I know of no other man who has contributed so much toward the co-ordination of efforts in gas turbine development, and who has done more to establish the delightful relations which have existed between the British and American workers in the field..."

For those services, the self-styled "betrayer" was awarded America's Medal of Freedom with Silver Palm. But before that honour, Dr Roxbee Cox was playing a central role in one of his greatest achievements.

"Before the War was over, there was a great deal of interest in Post-war education, particularly in aeronautics," he says. "In 1943 we *knew* we were going to win and should be preparing for the Post-war era.

"That summer, when I was Vice-president of the Royal Aeronautical Society, there was a huge two-day conference at which I took the chair and at which, broadly speaking, we discussed the education of the Post-war aeronautical elite. One of the moving spirits was Roy Fedden, who was working at the Ministry of Aircraft Production with the Minister, Sir Stafford Cripps.

"They produced this notion of a committee to make proposals for Post-war aeronautical education, and the outcome was the Fedden Committee, to which I gave evidence, and whose proposition was that there should be a College of Aeronautics.

"It was decided to begin work in 1945, and the first meeting of the Board of Governors of the College took place that year under the chairmanship of Air Chief Marshal Sir Edgar Ludlow-Hewitt. Our first task was, of course, to find a site for the college, recruit professors and lecturers and, ultimately, to collect the students.

"The first proposition for the site was Harwell, which was dropped for some reason, but of course the obvious place was the old Empire Test Pilots' School, which had all the appropriate adjuncts of an aeronautical centre. So we took that, and Cranfield started, very appropriately, with an airfield."

Those early days "were not without troubles. We had quite a search for the right kind of professors, but in the end recruited some extremely good people, and Ernest Relf, one of the initial members of the original Board, offered himself as the first Principal and made a perfectly good one.

"He was an extremely clever man who was head of the aerodynamics section of the National Physical Laboratory, and we got off to a fairly good start.

"His successor was Victor Goddard who, unfortunately, had a style which did not commend itself to Frederick Handley Page, who had succeeded as Chairman of the Board. They did not get on, and it was an uncomfortable period.

"Handley Page didn't like Goddard's style – I think there was perhaps too much of the Air Force officer about him. I don't know. I was a bit puzzled by it all, but when there were any arguments about administration, I was almost always with Handley Page. His point of view always seemed to be a sensible one.

"Anyway, there was a rumpus, at the end of which Victor Goddard resigned. We had a proper selection system for his successor, and fortunately chose Professor Alfred Murphy, who was Professor of Materials at the University of Birmingham, and who had also had experience in industry. There's no doubt he was a success, and we gradually built up a College of Aeronautics."

Looking back, Lord Kings Norton has no hesitation in pinpointing Cranfield's most significant year: "It was 1957, with the famous White Paper when Duncan Sandys was Air Minister. It said, in effect, 'We shan't want any pilots or aeronautics in future. It'll all depend on unmanned missiles'.

"It didn't quite put it like that, but the White Paper was a massive shock to us and the whole aircraft industry. It meant a different kind of Air Force, and it was a disturbing report and an idiotic one really. But it served as a warning to us that the future of aeronautics was not going to be as rosy as we had previously thought and that we had better find some means of diversifying.

"And that is what we did, diversifying into management, work systems and ultimately into mechanical engineering and combustion and so on. It was the beginning of the University scene, which we have now completely achieved, even to the extent of bringing in a medical element to what we are doing."

By the time of the diversification, Lord Kings Norton was Chairman of the Board of Governors, having succeeded Handley Page. "And when we became a University in 1969, we called ourselves the Cranfield Institute of Technology – and I personally would never have changed that.

"The trouble – and I admit this trouble – was that term Institute. With the Massachusetts and Californian Institutes of Technology, and the German and French Institutes, their nationals presumably understood what an Institute was. But when we say Institute, we think of the Women's Institute down the road!"

He laughs: "It's quite extraordinary, but Institute is not a term which is popular here. So ultimately we changed to University, and of course that was right. We are a

University. But the old term of Cranfield Institute of Technology is one I personally wished we had kept.

"We gained an enormous reputation with that title, quite rightly, because we have always been peculiar, in the sense that Cranfield is wholly post-graduate. We are odd, we are different. There's no place like us. The only other post-graduate school of comparable size is Imperial College, which is a really wonderful Institute – although, as a Fellow, I should perhaps declare an interest!

"The future? I don't think I can see anything different from a continuation of the present flow. I think we have got the right structure, although we will possibly develop on the biological side. There's probably more room in biotechnology than anywhere else.

"But it's extraordinary how aerodynamics develops, and even structures. I say 'even structures' because I had considerable experience of structural engineering in the Thirties, and the sort of limitations I saw then don't seem to have been barriers to progress, and it's quite amazing that we build aeroplanes bigger and bigger than people ever thought then.

"Having said that, there's a paper I did around 1940, or earlier, in which I discussed the size of aeroplanes, and I finished up with something pretty big. The curious thing is that although I was aware of the developments in jet propulsion, it was then all so secret that I couldn't bring them in.

"And one limiting factor in the way I was looking at it was, oddly enough, the span of the machine. Sticking to the present kind of configuration, the number of airscrews you could get in was defining the overall size. I finished up with almost 500 or 600 tons, and we're just about going beyond that now."

Despite that, forecasting the future is not a notion that appeals: "I think prophecy is a dangerous thing. I've done it once and I'll never do it again.

"In my Wright Lecture I was discussing the future, and of course forecast the civil airlines across the Atlantic, but didn't contemplate the gigantic increases in traffic there would be. And of course I did not really foresee the influences the War would have.

"The Americans were developing bombers while we were developing fighters, and that had a great Post-war influence, because obviously the airliners were likely to be developed from bombers. There again, we had been the experts in flying-boats before the War, and it could well have been that they were superior to the land-based aircraft. Then today's Heathrow might have been a series of canals!"

Whatever the outcome, Lord Kings Norton strongly believes Britain faces the same basic problem as she faced before the War: "Then we had a governing system, as we still have, which really cannot alter itself to take account properly of advancing science and technology.

"The reason we had plenty of Hurricanes during the War was because Tommy Sopwith, head of the Sopwith organisation, said 'We must have the things – never mind what the Ministry says!' And the reason the British aeronautical industry has had its hard times recently is largely through the faults of governments. They never know what to do about technology. It's quite extraordinary.

"I mean, you never find a government with engineers in it! They're all classical scholars, historians or modern language experts, and not one engineer or scientist.

"They have an advisory system – though whether they take advice or not I can't judge – but certainly the Government is not doing enough to support its most important industry, and that's the aircraft industry."

There are, he says, two aspects to the problem: "One is that engineers and scientists like being engineers and scientists and don't think it's a very good idea to do anything else. And the other is that it's recognised that if you're a history specialist, a Greek specialist, a Latinist or modern languages scholar, you can be what they call a generalist. And that it's a suitable training for running other people.

"But they don't admit that if you have a degree in engineering or engineering science or biology or some branch of physics, which would be more appropriate in these highly technical days, it's an equally good training for the mind to be a generalist."

It's a point made forcefully many times by Lord Kings Norton, who was knighted in 1953 and made a Life Peer in 1965. He recalls: "In 1948 I became Chief Scientist at the Ministry of Fuel and Power and was accorded the rank of Deputy Secretary – one step down from Permanent – and I was there for quite a while.

"But towards the end of my time I realised I would never be offered the job of Permanent Secretary. It was unheard of, and I decided to get out before I felt disappointed. I left Government service and changed course, and was making a success as a consultant and director of one or two companies.

"Then I was asked to be a member of the Scientific Manpower Committee, the chairman of which was my old chum Solly Zuckerman. We were discussing this very same thing, engineers and scientists not being in top administrative positions, and I said to Solly that I thought we should find out what were the basic disciplines of all our Permanent Secretaries. He said, 'You do that'.

"At that time there were 52 Permanent Secretaries, and I discovered that only one had other than what we call a humanitarian degree. He was a physicist – and he was Permanent Secretary of the Ministry of Pensions. At least when I spoke about that in the House of Lords, I was able to say we were now 100 per cent. better. We'd now got two!

"I suppose I don't despair because we always seem, somehow or other, to get away with it in the end. But we get no encouragement. To this day, every other country supports its aircraft industry to the full, but we don't. Of course the Ministry of Defence has to place contracts with the British Aerospace company, but it's not quite the same thing.

"The only aeroplane they've supported – and that was sadly belatedly – was Concorde, which of course was a howling success. And it's another British invention. The French may say they did it as well, but it was Archibald Russell who designed it and was persuaded by the French to make it a little smaller, which was a mistake.

Concorde: the fatigue tests were designed by Cranfield

"Even so, Concorde has been a tremendous success. I don't know of any other major aircraft which has done 20 years of service without an accident. But we haven't got very far with its successor.

"As I say, I have given up being a prophet, and I don't know what could happen next in supersonic flight. But in a way Concorde was only the beginning. There are bound to be more, but how it will be achieved, because of the terrible expense, I don't know.

"That is the difficulty we suffer from, more than other countries: investment in invention, or loyalty, is hard to come by. If you go to the City for money, the first thing they ask for is a history of profit, and if you've never built the thing before, how can you have a history of profit?

"I first flew in Concorde in 1972, and it didn't start making money until 10 or 12 years after that. So if you're going to go in for something really novel and expensive like that, you have to wait for your dividends.

"There are some things a financier can't wait for. He can't wait for up to 20 years for a return. But a government can, or ought to. That's where governments ought to come in, and if your government hasn't got that sort of vision, you are seriously handicapped."

On Cranfield and the future, Lord Kings Norton reflects: "I am a great believer in evolution, and if you've got a revolution you have to handle it extremely carefully. The

Whittle revolution was mishandled, but turned out to have been a major revolution. But big steps forward like that are rare, and you have to be very careful about how you handle them."

It is the voice of vast experience: "I have seen the whole thing," he says, "and it sometimes astonishes me." Not least the remarkable evolution of Cranfield, in which he has played such a major role.

"The progress of Cranfield has been phenomenal," he says. "I look back on its past with a great deal of pride and satisfaction, and I believe its future will be as remarkable as its past."